Fiscal Theory

Fiscal Theory

Government, Inflation, and Growth

Hans Brems
University of Illinois

LexingtonBooks
D.C. Heath and Company
Lexington, Massachusetts
Toronto

Library of Congress Cataloging in Publication Data

Brems, Hans.
 Fiscal theory.

 Includes index.
 1. Fiscal policy. 2. Inflation (Finance) 3. Monetary policy. 4. Economic
development.
 I. Title.
 HJ141.B73 1983   336.001   82-47905
 ISBN 0-669-05688-x

Published simultaneously in Canada

Printed in the United States of America

International Standard Book Number: 0-669-05688-x

Library of Congress Catalog Card Number: 82-47905

. . . taxes promote industry; not in consequence of their being raised upon individuals, but in consequence of their being expended by the state; that is, by increasing demand and circulation. —Sir James Steuart,
An Inquiry into the Principles of Political Economy

[Kings and ministers] are themselves always, and without any exception, the greatest spendthrifts in the society. Let them look well after their own expense, and they may safely trust private people with theirs.
—Adam Smith,
An Inquiry into the Nature and Causes of the Wealth of Nations

Contents

Figures

Tables

Preface

This book deals with topical issues but will emphasize analytical foundations rather than policy prescriptions. Its minor purpose is to restate Keynesian and monetarist orthodoxy and to trace early predecessors. Its major purpose is to offer a synthesis avoiding Keynesian as well as monetarist one-sidedness. To succeed, such a synthesis must use four equilibrating variables: the nominal rate of interest, physical output, the real rate of interest, and the rate of inflation. Such a synthesis must also include, but carefully distinguish between, the short and the long run.

For a quarter of a century we have possessed a simple and powerful model of long-run dynamics in R. M. Solow's neoclassical growth model. But this model had no policy handles, so its potential remained unexploited. Dealing with short-run unemployment, Keynesians obviously had no use for a long-run full-employment model. More surprisingly, monetarists have had no use for it either, although they habitually invoke the long run and exclude the rate of unemployment from their equilibrating variables.

Inflation and unemployment may, however, be put into the neoclassical growth model. In *Inflation, Interest, and Growth* (Lexington Books, 1980) I had taken some steps in that direction. When Stephen J. Turnovsky joined our department in 1981 I learned that he had added money, government, and taxes to the neoclassical growth model. By reading and conversation I have learned much from him.

This book began as a series of lectures given in Europe in the spring of 1982. For their hospitality I am indebted to the Industrial Institute for Economic and Social Research in Stockholm and to the Universities of Aarhus, Basel, Copenhagen, and Uppsala. For criticism and comment I am particularly indebted to Erik Gørtz of Copenhagen, Gunnar Thorlund Jepsen and Martin Paldam of Aarhus, and Gottfried Bombach and Christian Jäggi of Basel. Here at home I have benefited from numerous discussions with Donald R. Hodgman and Peter Birch Sørensen, a 1981–1982 visiting scholar. Henri Stegemeier helped me locate the Schiller quote in chapter 3. For clerical and photographic assistance I am grateful to the Department of Economics and the College of Commerce at the University of Illinois.

Acknowledgments

The author is indebted to:

The American Economic Association for permission to use, in chapter 7, passages from H. Brems, "Alternative Theories of Pricing, Distribution, Saving, and Investment, " *Amer. Econ. Rev.*, March 1979, *69*, 161–165.

The American Economic Association for permission to use, in chapter 8, two passages from Milton Friedman, "The Role of Monetary Policy," *Amer. Econ. Rev.*, March 1968, *58*, 1–17.

Lexington Books for permission to use, in chapters 3, 7, and 9, a few passages from chapters 1 and 6 of my previous Lexington Book, *Inflation, Interest, and Growth* (1980).

The Danish Economic Association for permission to use, in chapter 5, passages from H. Brems, "The Balanced Budget Revisited," in S. Andersen, K. Laursen, P. Nørregaard Rasmussen, and J. Vibe-Pedersen (eds.), *Economic Essays in Honour of Jørgen H. Gelting*, Copenhagen, 1982.

Princeton University Press for permission to use data from R. W. Goldsmith, *A Study of Saving in the United States I-III*, Princeton, 1955–1956, as reproduced by the U. S. Department of Commerce and shown in the lower half of figure 1–1 of the present book.

Introduction on Scope and Method

1. Scope

The commonly used term *monetary theory* refers to the theory of monetary policy. By analogy, the less commonly used term *fiscal theory* would refer to the theory of fiscal policy. The term *fiscal policy*, in turn, refers to government activities and their financing and has been so used in this book. But two clarifications are called for.

The first clarification is that, following tradition, we shall be dealing with less than the full fiscal policy. Macroeconomic tradition ignores transfer payments and their financing. The justification presumably is that economics deals with the allocation of output among the claims upon it. Macroeconomics summarily describes a threefold claim: households claim one part of national output for consumption; firms claim another for investment; and government claims a third part as government purchase of goods and services. Transfer payments seem less interesting. They are not a compensation for goods or services produced and hence are not part of either national product or national income. They are financed by what the government collects with one hand only to pay back with the other. They constitute no additional claim upon national output; they merely reshuffle the claims already mentioned. Via taxation or deficit financing somebody is enabled to consume more at the expense of somebody else's consumption or investment. If the reshuffling itself absorbs output, that claim has already been included in government purchase of goods and services.

The second clarification has to do with the line of demarcation between fiscal and monetary policy. Our economy will be a closed one in which money and bonds can come into existence in no other way than by financing a government budget deficit. Conversely, a government budget deficit can be financed in no other way than by expanding the money and bond supplies. We consider their rates of growth instruments of *fiscal* policy, and hence we are guilty of crossing the line of demarcation. But an inner sanctuary of monetary policy we shall always respect: given the rates of growth of the money and bond supplies, monetary policy is reduced to corrective action in two forms. First, by open-market operations in already existing old bonds, monetary policy may readjust the money and bond supplies, always expanding one at the expense of the other. Second, by varying reserve ratios, monetary policy may make Federal Reserve money go farther or shorter. We exclude all such corrective action from the scope of the present book and shall never mention it again.

Let us now turn from scope to method.

2. Specification and Operational Significance

Economists build models. Let the specification of an economic model refer to the number and functional form of the behavior hypotheses included in the model. We may think of three degrees of such specification.

The first and lowest degree—avoided in this book—is not even to say what the behavior hypotheses are. Such silence was common in the days of David Hume and survived in early monetarism, which relied on single-equation reduced-form econometrics. The idea of Friedman's "positive" economics was that if a reduced-form equation will fit the facts then never mind which particular behavior hypotheses it might be derived from. We, too, shall find reduced-form fitting (such as figure 8–1) useful, but only because it raises the question all science must raise: Why? Social science can answer that question only by offering hypotheses about human behavior.

The second degree of specification—also avoided in this book—is to enumerate behavior hypotheses without specifying their functional form. Each function is written with commas between its independent variables; the function is assumed to be differentiable; and the signs of its partial derivatives with respect to independent variables are specified. But no solutions, explicit or implicit, can ever be found from commas. At best, in special cases, the direction of the sensitivity of the unknown solution to economic policy may be found.

The third degree of specification—adopted in this book—is to specify the functional form of all behavior hypotheses. Solutions, explicit or implicit, may then be found and their sensitivities examined. All models to be presented in this book are solvable—and solved. Almost all solutions are explicit. By an explicit solution for a variable we mean an equation having that variable alone on one side and nothing but parameters on the other side. Each chapter of this book begins with a list of symbols carefully distinguishing variables from parameters.

Our third degree of specification does, however, expose the model builder to the objection that he is merely dealing with a special case—as special as, say, the Keynesian twin assumptions of a complete sensitivity of the demand for money and a complete insensitivity of the demand for investment to the rate of interest. Or as special as, say, the complete insensitivity of the demand for money to the rate of interest inherent in the vertical *LM* curve accepted by early monetarism and later abandoned, or the complete sensitivity of the rate of growth of the money wage rate to the rate of unemployment inherent in the vertical Phillips curve. We are not exempt from this objection, for we shall be dealing throughout the book with a closed economy, and we shall be dealing, in chapters 7 through 9, with steady-state equilibrium growth.

Operational significance refers to the richness of the solutions offered by the model. Obviously the better specified the behavior hypotheses are, the richer the solutions will be. But a high degree of operational significance is a property of the model itself and does not necessarily make the model more applicable. That brings us to the subject of true and false.

3. Validity and Applicability

Taking the outside world into account, let us think of the validity and applicability of an economic model as describing its realism. Validity refers to the extent to which behavior hypotheses are true in time and space. Applicability refers to the extent to which solutions will simulate historical or geographical reality.

The better specified the behavior hypotheses are, as we said, the richer the solutions will be. Well-specified behavior hypotheses and rich solutions are testable. But tests will prove them false if the model is merely dealing with special extreme cases such as those mentioned above. The model will lack validity and applicability!

The most common reason for lack of validity and applicability is the choice of assumptions or functional forms that keep certain variables from varying. If they cannot vary they cannot help equilibrating. Orthodox Keynesians fail to include the rate of inflation as an equilibrating variable and hence fail to distinguish between nominal and real rates of interest. Orthodox monetarists fail to include the rate of unemployment as an equilibrating variable.

This book tries to offer a synthesis avoiding Keynesian as well as monetarist special and extreme cases. To succeed, such a synthesis must meet two requirements. First, it must use at least four equilibrating variables: the nominal rate of interest, physical output, the real rate of interest, and the rate of inflation. Second, because Keynesians analyze the short run and monetarists the long run, a synthesis must include, but carefully distinguish between, the short and long run.

4. Statics and Dynamics

A static system determines the level of its variables at a particular time. Technically, a static system includes equations in which all variables refer to the same time and in which no derivatives with respect to time occur. The present book offers only one static system—the Keynesian system in chapter 4.

A dynamic system determines the time paths rather than the levels of its variables. Technically it does this by including either difference equations (relating a variable at one time to a variable at another) or differential equations (containing derivatives with respect to time). We prefer differential equations and use them in chapters 5 through 9. They are compact and neat, and their operation is greatly facilitated by the use of Euler's number e, the base of natural logarithms.

Our dynamics come in two stages. The short-run dynamics of chapters 5 and 6, called *semidynamics*, do not attempt to trace the effect of investment upon physical capital stock, to use a production function relating the flow of physical output to physical capital stock, or to optimize the latter. The long-run dynamics of chapters 8 and 9, called *full* dynamics, attempt to do those things.

5. Reading the Book

The book proceeds gently from the familiar and simple to the less familiar and simple. All chapters except chapter 6 are self-contained and may be read without reading any other chapter. Chapter 5 is the prerequisite for chapter 6.

If a model is to be solvable and solved it must include equations, and their functional form must be specified. Commas will not do! The book must use mathematics, then, and use them operationally. But the mathematics never go beyond elementary algebra and elementary differential and integral calculus.

Part I
The Setting

1

A Touch of
Fiscal History

1. Government Purchases of Goods and Services

In the United States, the growth of government purchases of goods and services has been roughly steady-state growth. The upper half of figure 1–1 shows total government purchases of goods and services in billions of constant dollars from 1870 to 1970. On the semilogarithmic scale used, the trend appears as a straight line. The two world wars represent the largest deviations from the trend. Each gave rise to a major deficit as shown in the lower half of the figure.

2. Financing the Deficit: United States and Germany

Government must finance deficits by issuing claims upon itself, either non-interest-bearing ones in the form of money or interest-bearing ones in the form of bonds.

The upper half of figure 1–2 shows the money supply in the United States in billions of current dollars between 1916 and 1970. The two major jumps occurred during the two world wars. The lower half of figure 1–2 shows net federal, state, and local government debt in the United States in billions of dollars for the same period. Here, too, the two major jumps occurred during the two world wars.

The German pictures are similar but more dramatic. For one thing, the very unit in which money is expressed changed twice! Figure 1–3 shows the currency supply in Germany in marks, reichsmarks, or deutsche marks during the 1910–1974 period. For another, the currency supply of 1923 was almost 10^{11} times larger than that of 1910! Even the generous scale adopted on the vertical axis of figure 1–3 cannot accommodate the 1923 currency supply of 4.96×10^{20}. The hyperinflation ended with the currency reform of November 1923, in which one new mark, to be called the reichsmark from 1924, was exchanged for 10^{12} old marks, called by Germans 1 billion old marks and by Americans 1 trillion old marks.

In a reduced territory and an impoverished economy after 1923, the currency supply was of the 1910 order of magnitude. Because of rigid price and wage controls, World War Two generated a mere tenfold increase in the currency supply—moderate by World War One standards. Like the hyper-

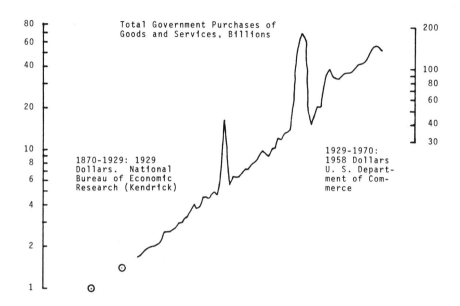

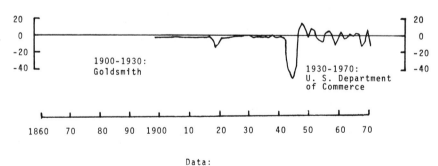

Data:

R. W. Goldsmith, *A Study of Saving in the United States,*
I-III, Princeton University Press, 1955-1956.

U. S. Department of Commerce, Bureau of Economic Analysis, *Long Term Economic Growth 1860-1970,* Washington, D.
C., 1973, 56.

Figure 1–1. Total Government Purchases of Goods and Services and Government Surplus or Deficit, United States, 1870–1970

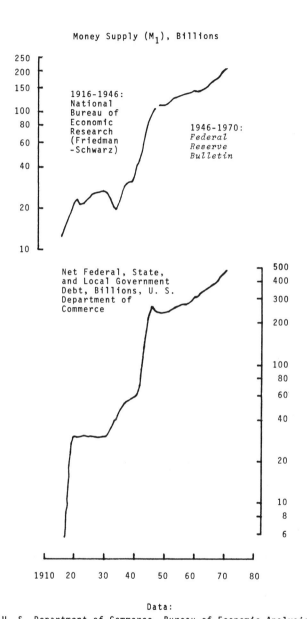

Money Supply (M$_1$), Billions

1916-1946:
National
Bureau of
Economic
Research
(Friedman
-Schwarz)

1946-1970:
*Federal
Reserve
Bulletin*

Net Federal, State,
and Local Government
Debt, Billions, U. S.
Department of
Commerce

Data:
U. S. Department of Commerce, Bureau of Economic Analysis,
Long Term Economic Growth 1860-1970, Washington, D. C. 1973,
57, 60.

Figure 1–2. Money Supply and Government Debt, United States, 1916–
1970

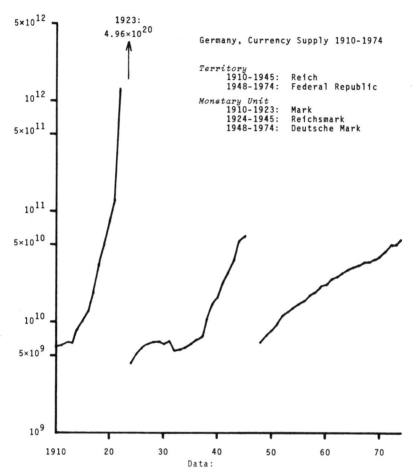

Germany, Currency Supply 1910-1974

Territory
  1910-1945:   Reich
  1948-1974:   Federal Republic

Monetary Unit
  1910-1923:   Mark
  1924-1945:   Reichsmark
  1948-1974:   Deutsche Mark

Data:

Deutsche Bundesbank, *Deutsches Geld- und Bankwesen in Zahlen 1876-1975,* Frankfurt am Main, 1976, 2 and 4.

Figure 1–3. Currency Supply, Germany, 1910–1974

inflation of the 1920–1923 period, the suppressed inflation between 1939 and 1948 ended with a currency reform. In an even more reduced territory, physically destroyed by aerial bombing, a currency supply of the 1910 order of magnitude was once again restored.

Figure 1–4 shows the federal debt in Germany in marks, reichsmarks, or deutsche marks from 1910 to 1974. The debt increased more than a thousandfold from the outbreak of World War One to the 1923 currency reform, which wiped out the entire war debt and then some. Again because of rigid price and wage controls, the debt increased less than a hundredfold

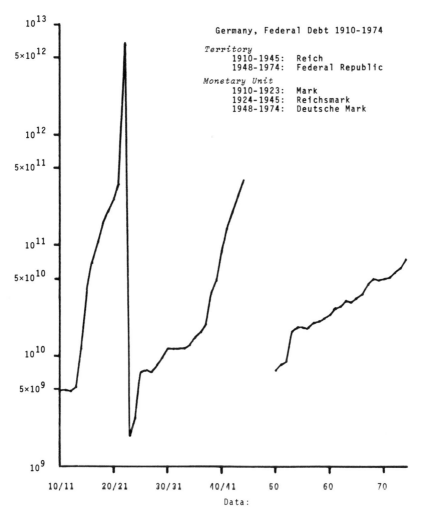

Deutsche Bundesbank, *Deutsches Geld- und Bankwesen in Zahlen 1876-1975*, Frankfurt am Main, 1976, 313-314.

Figure 1–4. Federal Debt, Germany, 1910–1974

during World War Two but was once again wiped out, this time in the currency reform of 1948.

From figures 1–1 through 1–4 we conclude that neither the United States nor Germany financed either of the world wars by taxes alone. The major deficits were financed both by issuing noninterest-bearing claims in the form of money and interest-bearing claims in the form of bonds. The real value of the resulting debt was eroded by inflation in the United States and wiped out by hyperinflation and currency reform in Germany.

3. Crowding Out and Crowding In

In a closed economy, if and only if the government budget is balanced will investment and saving be equal. Under a government deficit investment will fall short of savings and is in this sense being *crowded out*. Under a government surplus investment will exceed saving—might one call it being *crowded in*?

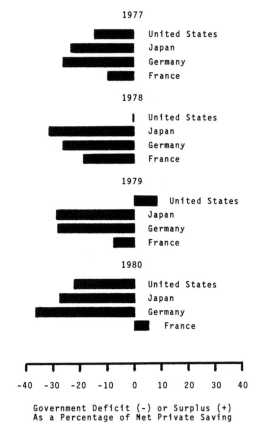

Figure 1–5. Crowding Out and Crowding In in the United States, Japan, Germany, and France, 1977–1980

In the late 1970s and 1980, government deficits in leading countries absorbed a significant part of net private saving. Defining net private saving as household saving plus business saving after capital consumption allowances, the OECD calculated government deficit $(-)$ or surplus $(+)$ as a percentage of net private saving for four leading countries in the 1977–1980 period as shown in figure 1–5.

Let us now turn to other aspects of recent history viewed through six macroeconomic functions.

2

Recent History as Experienced in Six Macroeconomic Functions

The seventeen years from 1965 through 1981 began with an escalation of a war setting off an inflation that was to accelerate from two to ten percent per annum over the first sixteen years—subsiding in 1971–1972 under price controls and in 1975–1976 under heavy excess capacity, refueled in 1972–1974 by oil, food, and decontrol shocks and in 1977–1979 by another oil shock, and finally subsiding again under the excess capacity in 1981–1982 helped by the collapsing oil cartel.

The story of such turbulence could be told as a qualitative chronology emphasizing policy measures adopted and discarded. Or the story could be told as a quantitative chronology tracing important variables as functions of time. The present chapter will do neither. Instead it will simply arrange the fourteen variables:

$C \equiv$ physical consumption
$g_P \equiv$ rate of inflation
$I \equiv$ physical net investment
$i \equiv$ interest payment per annum per government bond
$M \equiv$ supply of money
$P \equiv$ price of goods and services
$Q \equiv$ physical quantity of government bonds outstanding
$R \equiv$ government net receipts before interest paid by government
$r \equiv$ nominal rate of interest
$\rho \equiv$ real rate of interest
$X_{\max} =$ physical capacity
$X \equiv$ physical output
$Y \equiv$ money value of output
$y \equiv$ money disposable income

or ratios or differences between them and draw scatter diagrams of six macroeconomic behavior functions used by Keynes, Keynesians, or monetarists but all part of our tool kit. The chapter will simply try to form a rough impression of how well the six functions withstood the turbulence.

The chapter will use the *Economic Report of the President* transmitted to the Congress January 1982, supplemented by comments on concepts by Carson-Jaszi (1981) and de Leeuw (1979).

1.Inflation Tempered by Excess Capacity

Expecting inflation, firms will be compelled to contribute to it by raising their own price. But all price policy is a compromise between cost considerations and demand considerations: firms will be more reluctant to raise their own price at high excess capacity than at low excess capacity. Inflation, in other words, is tempered by excess capacity—but perhaps with a lag.

Price policy is part of a corporate routine requiring hearings of accounting, marketing, production, and finance staffs. Once reached, a decision will not be revised for some time. As a result, current-year price change could be expected to reflect previous-year rather than current-year excess capacity. Will it?

Figure 2–1 plots the rate of change of the gross-national-product fixed-weighted price index of the current year as a function of one minus the Wharton capacity utilization rate of the previous year. There is a visible short-run tendency for years having a high rate of excess capacity to induce next year a rate of inflation lower than that induced by years having a low rate of excess capacity. But no more than a short-run tendency is visible. The function comes, as it were, in layers. Three may be distinguished—1965–1970, 1971–1974, and 1975–1980. The two shifts may have been caused by the first and second oil shocks—in other words, by something external to the U.S. economy. Was a third shift on its way in 1981? The answer will be in only when this book is out. At press time in late 1982, however, the rate of inflation had been sharply reduced, and a third shift may not materialize.

2. Inflation and the Two Rates of Interest

After all, the corporate-bond yield is the yield of a nominal asset, whereas the common-stock yield tends to be the yield of a real one. As a first approximation, therefore, figure 2–2 uses the corporate-bond and the common-stock yields, respectively, as proxies for the nominal and real rates of interest and plots their difference as a function of the rate of change of the gross-national-product fixed-weighted price index. If the bond and stock yields were perfect representatives of the nominal and real rates of interest, respectively, their difference would always equal the rate of inflation, and all observations in a diagram like figure 2–2 would lie on a 45° line. Will they?

The observations of the first seven years stay very close to the 45° line, and so does the observation of 1976. But both oil shocks generated unprecedented rates of inflation, and the security markets apparently considered such rates temporary. Both when the rates turned out to be temporary—as in the 1975–1976 period—and when they did not—as in the 1980–1981 period—the security markets eventually returned to the immediate neigh-

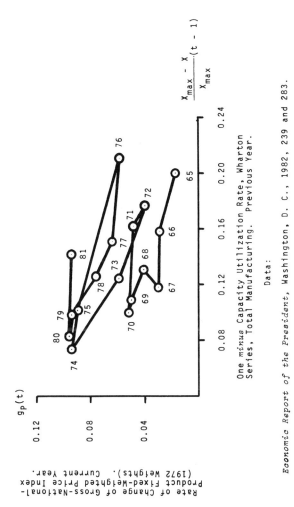

Figure 2–1. Inflation Tempered by Excess Capacity, United States, 1965–1981

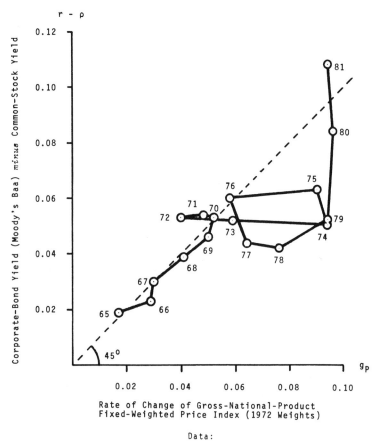

Data:

Economic Report of the President, Washington, D. C., 1982, 239, 310, and 337.

Figure 2–2. Inflation and the Two Rates of Interest, United States, 1965–
1981

borhood of the 45° line. In 1981 they even overshot. When all is said and done, there is a visible tendency for years with high rates of inflation to induce a gap between the nominal and real rate of interest; this gap is larger than that induced by years having a low rate of inflation.

3. Investment and the Real Rate of Interest

Physical net investment serves the purpose of expanding physical net national product X, hence will normally be growing at the same rate as the latter, leaving the ratio I/X the same. Only if net investment were a function of something else than X would the ratio I/X be varying. That something else could be the cost of capital, but which cost—the nominal or the real rate of interest? Physical investment is the acquisition of physical goods for the purpose of producing more such goods, and the price of the goods is growing at the rate of inflation. Consequently, investment would not be discouraged by a nominal rate of interest that was high merely because of inflation. Only a high real rate of interest would discourage investment—and perhaps with a lag.

Like price policy, investment policy is part of a corporate routine requiring time-consuming staff hearings. But a price-policy decision may at least be executed by the stroke of a pen. The execution of an investment-policy decision requires more time. Digging, construction, and delivery times will elapse before everything can be in place and appear as completed investment in the national income accounts. As a result, the current-year investment-product ratio could be expected to reflect a previous-year rather than a current-year real rate of interest. Will it?

Figure 2–3 plots the current-year ratio between net private domestic investment and net national product as a function of the previous-year common-stock yield. Figure 2–3 shows a visible tendency for years with a high real rate of interest to induce next year an investment-product ratio lower than that induced by years with a low real rate of interest. But no more than a tendency is visible. The first thirteen years from 1965 to 1977 cluster along a distinct beam, but the three years from 1978 to 1980 veer off the beam and display a higher investment-product ratio than one would have expected from real rates of interest as high as between 5 and 6 percent. Does the year 1981 hint a return to the pre-1978 beam?

4. A Consumption Function

Figure 2–4 is our venerable consumption function. Personal consumption expenditures in billions of 1972 dollars are plotted as a function of disposable personal income, also in billions of 1972 dollars. There is the familiar tendency for years with high disposable personal income to induce a personal consumption expenditure higher than that induced by years with low disposable personal income. As usual, but with the one exception of the first oil shock in 1973–1974, consumption and income are both monotonically rising.

5. A Tax-Revenue Function

Government gross receipts are defined as personal tax and nontax payments plus corporate profits tax liability plus indirect business tax and nontax

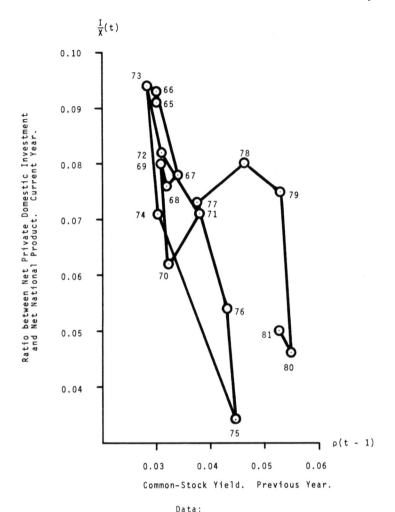

Figure 2-3. Investment and the Real Rate of Interest, United States, 1965–1981

Data:
Economic Report of the President, Washington, D. C., 1982, 233, 254, and 337.

liability plus contributions for social insurance. Subtract the part of government gross receipts paid back to the private economy in the form of transfer payments, subsidies, and interest paid by government and arrive at government net receipts. The part paid back to the private economy and thus netted out is a compensation for no goods or services produced; hence it is part of neither net national product nor national income.

May we ignore what is netted out—that is, what the government collects

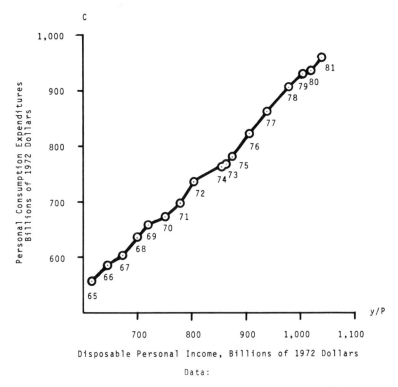

Figure 2-4. A Consumption Function, United States, 1965-1981

with one hand only to pay back with the other? We may if our focus is the dichotomy of government versus private. We may not if our focus is income redistribution or the incentive effects of transfer payments and taxes. The people from whom the government collects with one hand are not the same as those to whom the government pays back with the other.

The focus of this book is indeed the dichotomy of government versus private, so we may ignore the first two items netted out—that is, the transfer payments and subsidies. But the third item we may not ignore. In this book, the physical quantity Q of government bonds outstanding is an important policy instrument. Consequently interest paid by government iQ should appear visibly rather than being netted out. We must therefore define tax revenue R as government net receipts before interest paid by government— that is, as government gross receipts minus transfer payments minus subsidies.

Figure 2-5 plots tax revenue R thus defined as a function of net national product plus interest paid by government, $Y + iQ$. The former is virtually in

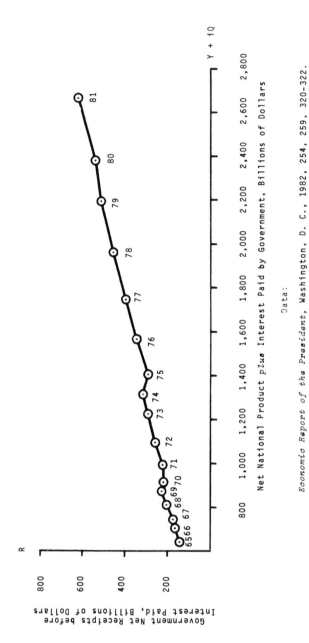

Data:

Economic Report of the President, Washington, D. C., 1982, 254, 259, 320–322.

Figure 2–5. A Tax-Revenue Function, United States, 1965–1981

proportion to the latter. The factor of proportionality is roughly 1/4. In other words, the U.S. tax system as a whole is neither progressive nor degressive. With the one exception of the first oil shock in 1974–1975, tax revenue R and net product plus interest paid $Y + iQ$ are both monotonically rising.

6. Velocity of Money and the Nominal Rate of Interest

Money M serves the purpose of transacting the money value Y of the net national product; hence it will normally be growing at the same rate as the latter, leaving the ratio Y/M the same. Only if the demand for money were a function of something else than Y would the ratio Y/M be varying. What does that ratio represent?

The money value Y of net national product is measured in dollars per annum, but the money supply M is measured in dollars. Dividing the former by the latter yields a flow-stock ratio having the dimension pure number per annum. That is nothing but the number of times per annum that money transacts product—that is, the velocity of money.

What could that something else than Y be of which the demand for money were a function? It could be the cost of holding money, but which cost, the nominal or the real rate of interest? The opportunity cost of holding money in noninterest-bearing liquid form is the nominal rate of interest it could earn in an interest-bearing form. So if the nominal rate of interest were up, money would be more expensive to hold, and firms and households could be expected to try to hold less of it by making it circulate more rapidly. Will they?

Figure 2–6 measures the velocity of money as the ratio between net national product and the money supply M1. The latter, in turn, is defined as currency plus demand deposits, travelers' checks, and other checkable deposits at banks and thrift institutions. Figure 2–6 plots the velocity of money thus measured as a function of the nominal rate of interest represented by the corporate-bond yield.

There is a visible tendency for years with a high nominal rate of interest to induce a velocity of money higher than that induced by years with a low nominal rate of interest. But no more than a tendency is visible. Like figure 2–1, figure 2–6 comes, as it were, in three layers: 1965–1972, 1973–1976, and 1977–1981. The velocity of money is a matter of habits of payments, and habits change slowly.

7. Conclusion

With a minimum of technique we have drawn two-dimensional scatter diagrams of six macroeconomic functions: a Phillips function, a two-rates-

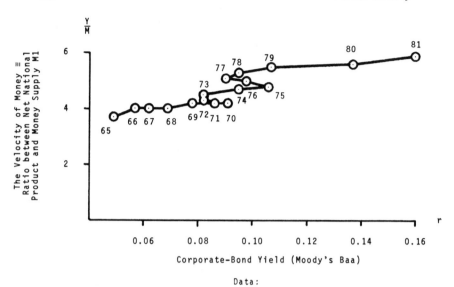

Data:
Economic Report of the President, Washington, D. C., 1982, 254, 303, and 310.

Figure 2-6. Velocity of Money and the Nominal Rate of Interest, United
States, 1965-1981

of-interest function, an investment function, a consumption function, a
tax-revenue function, and a velocity-of-money function.

The scatters form beams of widely differing width. But even the narrow-
est beams, those of the consumption and tax-revenue functions, show the
powerful impact of the food and oil shocks.

In chapters 5 and 6 we shall use simplified—linearized—macroeconomic functions like the six just examined to build fiscal-policy models of a
nonaccommodating as well as an accommodating fiscal policy.

References

C.S. Carson and G. Jaszi, "The National Income and Products Accounts of
the United States: An Overview," *Survey of Current Business*, Feb.
1981, 22-34.

F. de Leeuw, "Why Capacity Utilization Estimates Differ," *Survey of
Current Business*, May 1979, 45-55.

U.S. Government, *Economic Report of the President*, Washington, D.C.,
1982.

3 Early Macroeconomic Theory: Unemployment and Inflation

Körper und Stimme leiht die Schrift dem stummen Gedanken, Durch der Jahrhunderte Strom trägt ihn das redende Blatt.[1]
—Friedrich Schiller, "Der Spaziergang" (1795)

Economic theory may be seen in three dimensions. First, its subject matter may be quantity or price. Second, its degree of aggregation may be macro or micro. The first two dimensions give us a simple two-by-two matrix shown in table 3–I. A third dimension—in which each of the four areas of table I may be seen—is the time reference of economic theory. A static model determines the levels of its variables at a particular time. A dynamic model determines the time paths rather than the levels of its variables.

These three dimensions may help us visualize, say, the following nine major phases in the development of economic theory over the past three centuries:

1. Seventeenth-century unemployment theory: the mercantilists.
2. Eighteenth-century static inflation theory: Hume and Smith's formulation of Say's Law.
3. Eighteenth-century allocation and relative-price theory: the physiocrat land theory of value, sectoral interdependence, and circular flow.
4. Early nineteenth-century relative-price theory: the classical labor theory of value.
5. Late nineteenth-century allocation and relative-price theory: the Walrasian theory of general economic equilibrium.
6. Turn-of-the-century dynamic inflation theory: Wicksell and Fisher.

Table 3–I
Two Dimensions of Economic Theory

	Macro	*Micro*
Quantity	Unemployment theory	Allocation theory
Price	Inflation theory	Theory of relative prices

7. Early twentieth-century unemployment theory: Ohlin and Keynes.
8. Twentieth-century dynamics: Post-Keynesian and neoclassical steady-state growth.
9. Late twentieth-century dynamic inflation theory: the monetarists.

The present book will confine itself to macroeconomics. Macroeconomics is the branch of economics interested in the aggregated volume of output rather than its composition and in the price level rather than relative prices. In practice, macroeconomic models imagine an economy producing a single good. Here physical output as well as price are well-defined variables expressible as single numbers.

Simple algebra and simple estimation are welcome results of such crude simplification. A less-welcome result is the greater scope for subjectivity. Simplifying means leaving things out of account, and for three centuries theorists have failed to agree on which particular things are too important to be left out. Some say quantity, some say price. Two schools of thought may be said to have asserted themselves with varying weights over the centuries. They are unemployment theory and inflation theory, respectively.

The present chapter traces Keynesian unemployment theory back to Sir William Petty, Thomas Mun, Andrew Yarranton, Sir James Steuart, James Maitland Lauderdale, and Bertil Ohlin and traces monetarist inflation theory back to David Hume, Anne Robert Jacques Turgot, Jean Baptiste Say, David Ricardo, Knut Wicksell, and Irving Fisher.

I. Unemployment Theory

Unemployment theory is the oldest of the two schools. Here, physical output is seen as bounded by demand. Supply is no problem: demand will create its own supply. There is always excess capacity. Monetary or fiscal policy may stimulate demand, and the result will be larger physical output and better utilization of resources. In its extreme form the school has ideological overtones: left to itself, capitalism is incapable of utilizing its own resources. Government action is the remedy.

Economics, a latecomer among sciences, emerged together with the nation-state in the seventeenth century. Its practitioners were advisers, invited or uninvited, to the absolute monarch. The monarch wanted to know how to finance the mercenaries of his wars, the splendor of his court, the sciences and the arts, and his subsidies to new industries.

But there was more to seventeenth-century economics than the narrow problem of public finance. Technological progress in agriculture had released labor and generated unemployment.

1. Seventeenth-Century Unemployment Theory:
The Mercantilists, Fiscal Policy

In a neat piece of sector analysis Sir William Petty [1662(1899:30)] estimated unemployment as follows. Out of a total labor force of 1,000, on an average of good and bad years only 900 will be employed—100 in agriculture; 200 in export; 400 in luxuries ("the ornaments, pleasure, and magnificence of the whole"); and 200 in the service industries ("Governours, Divines, Lawyers, Physicians, Merchants, and Retailers"). The remaining 100 would be unemployed:

> the question is, since there is food enough for this supernumerary 100 also, how should they come by it? whether by begging or by stealing; . . . perhaps they may get either by begging or stealing more than will suffice them, which will for ever after indispose them to labour. . . .

Petty's remedy was public works satisfying two conditions. The first condition was high labor intensity. The works should be "works of much labour, and little art" (1899:30). The second condition was low import requirement: "let it be without expence of Foreign Commodities" (1899:31). With these two conditions satisfied, public works should preferably be productive:

> making all High-wayes so broad, firm, and eaven, as whereby the charge and tedium of travelling and Carriages may be greatly lessened. The cutting and scowring of Rivers into Navigable; the planting of usefull Trees for timber, delight, and fruit in convenient places (1899:29).

But to Petty, productivity was not the prime consideration:

> 'tis no matter if it be employed to build a useless Pyramid upon *Salisbury Plain*, bring the Stones at *Stonehenge* to *Tower-Hill*, or the like; for at worst this would keep their mindes to discipline and obedience, and their bodies to a patience of more profitable labours when need shall require it (1899:31).

So much for fiscal policy.

2. Seventeenth-Century Unemployment Theory:
The Mercantilists, Monetary Policy

Public works were one way of employing the unemployed; private investment was another. Private investment would be encouraged by a low rate of interest. To Petty, the rate of interest was determined by the money supply, and to Petty, money was metal. Now under a metal standard where does money come from? Thomas Mun [1664(1856:135)] gave the simple answer:

> I will take that for granted which no man of judgment will deny, that we have no other means to get Treasure but by forraign trade, for Mines wee have none which do afford it . . . mony is gotten . . . by making our commodities which are exported yearly to over ballance in value the forraign wares which we consume. . . .

In England money was metal, but Andrew Yarranton [1677(1854:38)] called attention to the practice of Dutch banks of extending credit with mortgages as collateral:

> Observe all you that read this, and tell to your children this strange thing, that *paper in Holland is equal with moneys in England.* . . .

and believed that following the Dutch example would lower the rate of interest from 6 to 4 percent.

3. Were They Keynesians?

Keynes (1936:336) did not think of himself as the first Keynesian but found mercantilist reasoning compatible with his own:

> At a time when the authorities had no direct control over the domestic rate of interest . . . the effect of a favourable balance of trade on the influx of the precious metals was their only *indirect* means of reducing the domestic rate of interest and so increasing the inducement to home investment.

Was Keynes, the theorist, putting words into the mouths of the mercantilists? Heckscher (1955:353), the historian, thought so. The real reason, he said, for the excess of currency so characteristic of the history of Western civilization, was simply that governments needed money to finance wars and other state expenditures. In Heckscher's judgment, the effects on general economic life might have materialized but were generally not intended. To Keynes the mercantilists had a Keynesian model; to Heckscher they were pragmatists.

4. A Balanced Budget Multiplier: Steuart (1767)

Immediately before Adam Smith, mercantilism found a late codifier in Sir James Steuart [1767(1796:271–272)]. Taxes, he said, were expansionary, because they reduced taxpayer's demand by less than they increased government demand:

> In proportion . . . as taxes draw money into circulation, which otherwise would not have entered into it at that time, they encourage industry; not by taking the money from individuals, but by throwing it into the hands of the state, which spends it. . . .

> It is no objection to this representation of the matter, that the persons from whom the money is taken, would have spent it as well as the state. The answer is, that it might be so, or not: whereas when the state gets it, it will be spent undoubtedly.

With Steuart's distinction between the propensities to consume of taxpayers and government, the balanced-budget multiplier was ready for formalization. But the times became unfavorable to interventionist views, and the formalization had to wait for 174 years before it was accomplished by Gelting (1941) and Haavelmo (1945) within a straight Keynesian framework of a single equilibrating variable—that is, physical output.

5. Debt Management: Lauderdale (1804)

A few English classicists, too, were concerned with oversaving and unemployment. James Maitland Lauderdale was, perhaps, the most clear-headed among them.

The government budget constraint is usually applied to the case of fiscal deficits. But to understand Lauderdale, we must run it in reverse and apply it to a fiscal surplus. Thus applied, it says that a government surplus may be financed in two ways. Either the government destroys noninterest-bearing claims upon itself called money, or the government buys back interest-bearing claims upon itself called bonds. The government budget constraint will still be of the form to be used in chapters 5, 6, and 9. That is

$$GP + iQ - R = \frac{dM}{dt} + \Pi \frac{dQ}{dt} \qquad (3.1)$$

where

$G \equiv$ physical government purchase of goods and services
$i \equiv$ interest payment per annum per government bond
$M \equiv$ supply of money
$P \equiv$ price of goods and services
$\Pi \equiv$ price of bonds
$Q \equiv$ physical quantity of government bonds outstanding

$R \equiv$ tax revenue
$t \equiv$ time

Between "the glorious revolution" of 1688—establishing the rule of William and Mary—and 1804, the British public debt had grown almost a thousandfold, from 0.66 million to 556 million pound sterling [Alvin Hansen (1951:230)]. Debt management was widely discussed, and the government planned, upon the return of peace, to run fiscal surpluses large enough to buy back its own bonds and retire the entire debt in forty-five years. In other words, the dQ/dt part of the budget constraint 3.1 was under debate.

Lauderdale saw such rapid retirement in terms of what Keynesians would call the consumption function and the marginal efficiency of capital. Huge tax collections would lower the consumption function and put huge sums into the hands of bondholders. Would the bondholders be disposed to consume those sums? No way, said Lauderdale (1804:245–246):

> it would have been difficult to persuade the proprietors of stock . . . all at once to spend, as revenue, that which habit had taught them to regard as capital. . . .

Now if the bondholders were not disposed to consume them, the sums would become investment-seeking funds at the very moment investment outlets were being closed by the depressed consumption (265–266):

> the continued progress of accumulation . . . increases the quantity of capital; whilst, far from increasing, (by . . . abridging consumption), it inevitably diminishes the demand for it.

Lauderdale may have been the first to use the government budget constraint 3.1 but did not write it algebraically. The first to do so was probably Bent Hansen (1955:chapter III). Ott and Ott (1965) and Christ (1967) were the first to show that a macroeconomic model becomes dynamic once it incorporates the government budget constraint. Their budget constraint failed to include the payment of interest iQ on government bonds. The complete constraint 3.1 was offered by Blinder and Solow (1974) and Turnovsky (1977).

6. Early Twentieth-Century Unemployment Theory:
Ohlin and Keynes

Immediately preceding Keynes, the most complete anticipation was Bertil Ohlin's. Ohlin (1934) used four Keynesian tools of analysis: physical output as a variable, the propensity to save, liquidity preference, and the multiplier.

His Keynesian tools led him to Keynesian policy conclusions. One of them was that in times of excess capacity, the government should undertake investment projects—say highway construction or the electrification of state railroads—that would not compete with private investment and that should be allowed to generate fiscal deficits. Tax financing would reduce consumption and thus defeat the purpose of public works. Ohlin wrote the verbal counterpart to our government budget constraint 3.1: such deficits may be financed by expanding either the money or the bond supply. Sale of government bonds, Ohlin said, would depress bond prices and thus discourage private investment, again defeating the purpose of public works. That left central-bank discounting of treasury bills as the only way which would not deprive private investment of finance. Thus financed, public works would generate income, and the income generation would be magnified by the multiplier.

For all their similarities, there was an important difference between Ohlin and Keynes. Ohlin was rooted in the Wicksellian tradition (Wicksell is described later in this chapter). To the Wicksellian Ohlin, physical output was as variable as it was to be to Keynes (1936) two years later. But Ohlin's feedback between physical output and aggregate demand was not telescoped into an instant static equilibrium along a physical-output axis, as the Keynesian one was to be. Ohlin's feedback unfolds in a cumulative process along a time axis, as did the Wicksellian one between prices and aggregate demand. In short, Ohlin used dynamics, Keynes statics.

7. Summary of Unemployment School

Mainstream mercantilists, their codifier Steuart, the classicist Lauderdale, and the Wicksellian Ohlin anticipated elements of a Keynesian equilibrium in which physical output and the rate of interest are the equilibrating variables in the goods and money markets, respectively. Prices are, in effect, frozen and ignored. Diagnosis: The propensity to consume may be too low and the inducement to invest too weak to allow full employment. Prescription: Monetary policy may expand the money supply, depress the rate of interest, and strengthen the inducement to invest. Fiscal policy may reduce tax rates and thus stimulate consumption. Fiscal policy may finance public works by deficit spending and thus generate new income.

II. Inflation Theory

Inflation theory emerged in the eighteenth century. Here, physical output is seen as bounded by supply. Demand is no problem: supply will create its own demand. There is never excess capacity. Monetary or fiscal policy may stimulate demand but to no use: monetary stimuli will merely generate inflation, fiscal stimuli merely crowding out. In its extreme form the school has ideological overtones: left to itself, capitalism is fully capable of utilizing its own resources. Government action, however well meant, is the problem.

1. Eighteenth-Century Static Inflation Theory: Hume

No static model can determine anything else than the level of its variables. David Hume (1752) unfroze price within a static framework, simply asking how high prices would be. His answer was a strict proportionality between prices and the money supply:

> Suppose four-fifth of all the money in *Great Britain* to be annihilated in one night . . . what would be the consequence? Must not the price of all labour and commodities sink in proportion. . . . ?
>
> Again, suppose that all the money of *Great Britain* were multiplied fivefold in a night, must not the contrary effect follow?

In conclusion, Mun's, Petty's, or Yarranton's prescriptions would not work. Neither a positive balance of trade bringing in more precious metals nor an expansion of mortgage-backed bank credit could have any effect other than inflation; hence both would be redundant as well as harmful. Hume's prescription: keep the money supply under control.

2. Say's Law

Formally no part of a quantity theory of money, Say's Law was a neat supplement to it. Say's Law explained why monetary expansion was redundant: supply would always create its own demand.

Say's Law did not have to wait for Say (1803). It comes in two installments, and Smith (1776) had both. The first installment is the national product-national income identity. Generation of product is generation of value added. To the firm, value added is either cost or profit; to the worker, landlord, and capitalist, the cost of hiring their services is their income. Consequently national product and national income are the same thing seen from two different angles, hence are by definition identical. Adam Smith [1776(1805:204)] said it succinctly:

> the annual revenue of every society is always precisely equal to the ex-

changeable value of the whole annual produce of its industry, or rather is precisely the same thing with that exchangeable value.

Modern economists doubt neither that product and income are the same thing nor that income is a necessary condition for demand. But is it also a sufficient condition? If income is taxed, private demand is curtailed, and will government demand always fill the gap? As we saw, Steuart (1767) discussed that question. If income is saved, consumption is curtailed, and will investment demand always fill the gap? That brings us to the second installment.

The second installment of Say's Law says that what is saved is always invested. Smith (1805:78–79) expressed it as follows:

> Whatever a person saves from his revenue he adds to his capital, and either employs it himself in maintaining an additional number of productive hands, or enables some other person to do so, by lending it to him for an interest. . . .

> What is annually saved is as regularly consumed as what is annually spent, and nearly in the same time too; but it is consumed by a different set of people.

Whereas Smith had both installments of Say's Law, Say himself [1803 (1814:147)] had only the first one:

> Il est bon de remarquer qu'un produit créé offre, *dès cet instant*, un débouché à d'autres produits pour tout le montant de sa valuer. . . .[2]

Once earned, would income become demand? Say (1814:147) had no doubts that it would, but his words are an assertion rather than a demonstration:

> L'argent ne remplit qu'un office passager dans ce double échange; et les échanges terminés, il se trouve toujours qu'on a payé des produits avec des produits.[3]

Say's friend and colleague, Ricardo [1817(1951:290)] agreed:

> No man produces, but with a view to consume or sell, and he never sells, but with an intention to purchase some other commodity, which may be immediately useful to him, or which may contribute to future production. By producing, then, he necessarily becomes either the consumer of his own goods, or the purchaser and consumer of the goods of some other person.

Doubts were expressed by Marx [1904(1923:276)]:

Das Geld ist nicht nur "das Medium, wodurch der Austausch bewirkt wird," sondern zugleich das Medium, wodurch der Austausch von Produkt gegen Produkt in zwei Akte zerfällt, die von einander unabhängig und räumlich und zeitlich getrennt sind. . . .[4]

The doubts persisted in Keynes but were questioned by Patinkin (1956), whose real-balance effect may be seen as a rehabilitation of Say's Law, as we shall do in chapter 4.

3. Turn-of-the-Century Dynamic Inflation Theory: Wicksell

Hume had described what would happen to prices if "all the money of *Great Britain* were multiplied fivefold in a night" but failed to describe how all that money would find its way into the economy. Ricardo [1817(1951:364)] saw how:

The applications to the bank for money, then, depend on the comparison between the rate of profits that may be made by the employment of it, and the rate at which they are willing to lend it.

Wicksell [1898(1936)] restated Ricardo's idea within a framework of which three characteristics are worth remembering. First, Wicksell defined a "natural" rate of interest as the marginal productivity of capital at prices expected to remain stationary. By confronting the natural rate with the "money" rate of interest charged by banks, Wicksell broke the barrier between capital theory and monetary theory and identified the mechanism through which the new money would find its way into the economy: a money rate falling short of the natural rate will encourage a demand for money which can be met only by expanding the money supply. Wicksell [1906(1935:193,201)] emphasized this effect by defining a third rate of interest, the "normal" one, as the rate that could equalize saving and investment and presumably require no expansion of the money supply. A money rate falling short of the natural rate will generate inflation. Wicksell [1898(1936:102)] emphasized this effect by defining a fourth rate of interest, the "neutral" one, as the rate which would keep prices stationary. Is a normal rate of interest also a neutral one? Wicksell thought so. Second, Wicksell's framework employed such modern concepts as aggregate demand and supply. Third, because Wicksell wanted to deal with inflation, and because inflation is defined as the proportionate rate of growth of price, he needed a dynamic model. He carefully built one. He dated his variables, emphasized the timing of events, and offered a step-by-step account of how the new money finds its way into the economy. His dynamics were preserved in Ohlin's unemployment theory but lost in the Keynesian revolution.

4. Turn-of-the-Century Dynamic Inflation Theory: Fisher

Any model admitting inflation as an equilibrating variable will immediately have two additional ones—the nominal and the real rate of interest.

Just as we ran the government budget constraint in reverse and applied it to the case of a fiscal *surplus* to understand Lauderdale, we shall have to run the distinction between a nominal and a real rate of interest in reverse and apply it to the case of *deflation* to understand Fisher. Writing in the closing years of the price decline of the last quarter of the nineteenth century, Fisher (1896:8–9) distinguished between a rate of interest in gold (the nominal rate of interest) called i and a rate of interest in wheat (the real rate of interest) called j. Calling the rate of appreciation of gold in terms of wheat a, he wrote

$$1 + j = (1 + a)(1 + i) \tag{3.2}$$

In other words, in the case of deflation the real rate of interest j would be greater than the nominal rate i.

Wicksell [1898(1936:165–166)] knew Fisher's work and reversed it from the case of deflation to the case of inflation: "entrepreneurs incur their 'expense' (wages, rents, etc.) when things are cheap, and dispose of their product after prices have gone up." Strangely enough Wicksell was unimpressed: "Such a rise in prices . . . does not provide [the entrepreneurs] with the means of paying a higher rate of interest." Wicksell must have identified himself with his entrepreneurs who would never anticipate such a rise in prices, because they always expect current prices to prevail in the future. Rational expectations were not yet in vogue!

A glimpse of the distinction between nominal and real interest was, perhaps, caught more than two centuries ago by Anne Robert Jacques Turgot [1769–1770(1844:49)]:

> la cause même qui augmente la quantité de l'argent au marché et qui augmente le prix des autres denrées en baissant le prix de l'argent soit précisément celle qui augmente le loyer de l'argent ou le taux de l'interêt.[5]

5. Late Twentieth-Century Dynamic Inflation
Theory: Monetarism

Hume, Turgot, Say, Wicksell, and Fisher may be seen as forerunners of a monetarist model of inflation in which the equilibrating variables are three rates: the rate of inflation, the nominal rate of interest, and the real rate of interest—but not a fourth one, the rate of unemployment.

Do extreme monetarists wish to revive Hume's strict proportionality between prices and the money supply? If monetarists wish to travel all the way back to 1752, some severe surgery would be necessary.

First, if the demand for money is lower when the rate of interest is higher, the velocity of money is higher when the rate of interest is higher. If so, Hume's strict proportionality would be lost. It could be restored only by assuming a complete insensitivity of the demand for money to the rate of interest, as Friedman once (1959) did but no longer (1966,1972) does.

Second, the rate of growth of the money wage rate would have to be completely sensitive to the rate of unemployment. Otherwise, a larger money supply would not be entirely absorbed by higher prices but would be partly dissipated in reduced unemployment, and again Hume's strict proportionality would be lost. It could be restored only by a vertical Phillips curve (1958)—ruling out the rate of unemployment as an equilibrating variable, as Friedman (1968) does.

With that done, the monetarist diagnosis is simple. There is inflation, because the money supply is growing too rapidly. Prescription against inflation: keep the money supply under control. Prescription against unemployment: none, and none is called for. In the long run, the rate of unemployment will seek its "natural" level regardless of monetary or fiscal policy.

III. Keynesians and Monetarists Compared

If answers differ as strikingly as those offered by Keynesians and monetarists, one wonders if the same question is being answered. The impression is left by Friedman (1970) that the two schools use much the same *IS-LM* framework. Merely parameter estimates would differ; each school would emphasize certain sensitivities and ignore others. A more fundamental difference is that, since Steuart and Lauderdale, fiscal policy has always been important to Keynesians but ignored by Friedman.

Perhaps the most fundamental difference between Keynesians and monetarists is simply that the former analyze the short run and the latter the long one. We shall divide the present book accordingly. Part II will deal with the short run, beginning with Keynesian statics and proceeding to a semi-dynamic treatment of four equilibrating variables. We make no attempt to trace the effect of investment on physical capital stock, use a production function relating the flow of physical output to physical capital stock, or optimize the latter.

Part III will deal with the long run, simulating monetarism within the framework of a neoclassical growth model and proceeding to a full model of a steady-state growth. As Hahn and Matthews (1964) did, we define steady-state growth as stationary proportionate rates of growth. Part III will indeed attempt to trace the effect of investment upon physical capital stock, use a production function relating the flow of physical output to physical capital stock, and optimize the latter.

Notes

1. "Scripture lends body and voice to unspoken thought, The articulate page conveys it through the passage of centuries" (my translation.)
2. "It is well worth mentioning that the very moment it is completed, a product offers a market for other products to the full amount of its own value" (my translation.)
3. "Money merely plays a transitory role in this double exchange, and once the exchanges have been completed it will always be found that products have been paid with products" (my translation.)
4. "Money is not merely 'the medium accomplishing the exchange' but also the medium breaking up the exchange into two acts, independent of each other and separated in space and time" (my translation.)
5. "The very cause which augments the quantity of money in the market and raises the price of other goods, thus reducing the value of money, is precisely the one which raises the rental of money—that is, the rate of interest" (my translation.)

References

A. S. Blinder and R. M. Solow, "Analytical Foundations of Fiscal Policy," *The Economics of Public Finance* (Brookings), Washington, D.C., 1974.
C. F. Christ, "A Short-Run Aggregate-Demand Model of the Interdependence and Effects of Monetary and Fiscal Policies with Keynesian and Classical Interest Elasticities," *Amer. Econ. Rev.*, May 1967, *57*, 434–443.
I. Fisher, "Appreciation and Interest," *Publications of the American Economic Association*, Aug. 1896, *11*, 331–442.
M. Friedman, "The Demand for Money: Some Theoretical and Empirical Results," *J. Polit. Econ.*, Aug. 1959, *67*, 327–351.
———, "Interest Rates and the Demand for Money," *J. Law Econ*, Oct. 1966, *9*, 71–85.
———, "The Role of Monetary Policy," *Amer. Econ. Rev.*, Mar. 1968, *58*, 1–17.
———, "A Theoretical Framework for Monetary Analysis," *J. Polit. Econ.*, March/April 1970, *78*, 193–238.
———, "Comments on the Critics," *J. Polit. Econ.*, Sept.–Oct. 1972, *80*, 906–950.

J. Gelting, "Nogle bemaerkninger om finansieringen af offentlig virksomhed," *Nationaløkonomisk Tidsskrift*, 1941, *79*, 293–299.

T. Haavelmo, "Multiplier Effects of a Balanced Budget," *Econometrica*, Oct. 1945, *13*, 311–318.

F. H. Hahn and R. C. O. Matthews, "The Theory of Economic Growth: A Survey," *Econ. J.*, Dec. 1964, *74*, 779–902.

A. H. Hansen, *Business Cycles and National Income*, New York, 1951.

B. Hansen, *Finanspolitikens ekonomiska teori*, Stockholm, 1955, translated as *The Economic Theory of Fiscal Policy*, London, 1958; Lund, 1967.

E. F. Heckscher, *Mercantilism*, London, 1955.

D. Hume, "Of the Balance of Trade," *Political Discourses*, Edinburgh, 1752.

J. M. Keynes, *The General Theory of Employment, Interest, and Money*, London, 1936.

J. M. Lauderdale, *An Inquiry into the Nature and Origin of Public Wealth and into the Means and Causes of its Increase*, Edinburgh and London, 1804.

K. Marx, *Theorien über den Mehrwert*, K. Kautsky (ed.), Stuttgart, 1904; Berlin, 1923.

T. Mun, *England's Treasure by Forraign Trade*, London, 1664, reprinted in J.R. McCulloch (ed.), *A Select Collection of Early English Tracts on Commerce*, London, 1856.

B. Ohlin, *Penningpolitik, offentliga arbeten, subventioner och tullar som medel mot arbetslöshet*, Stockholm, 1934.

D. J. Ott and A. Ott, "Budget Balance and Equilibrium Income," *J. Finance*, March 1965, *20*, 71–77.

W. Petty, *A Treatise of Taxes and Contributions*, London, 1662; reprinted in C. H. Hull (ed.), *The Economic Writings of Sir William Petty*, Cambridge, 1899.

A. W. Phillips, "The Relation between Unemployment and the Rate of Change of Money Wage Rates in the United Kingdom, 1861–1957," *Economica*, Nov. 1958, *25*, 283–299.

D. Ricardo, *Principles of Political Economy and Taxation, Works and Correspondence*, P. Sraffa (ed.), *I*. Cambridge, 1951.

J. B. Say, *Traité d'economie politique*, Paris, 1803; second edition, 1814.

A. Smith, *An Inquiry into the Nature and Causes of the Wealth of Nations*, Edinburgh, 1776; "new" edition, Glasgow, 1805.

J. Steuart, *An Inquiry into the Principles of Political Economy*, London, 1767, 1796.

A. R. J. Turgot, "Réflexions sur la formation et la distribution des richesses," *Ephémérides du citoyen*, Nov. 1769–Jan. 1770; reprinted in E. Daire (ed.), *Oeuvres de Turgot*, Paris, 1844; translated as *Reflections on the Formation and the Distribution of Riches*, New York, 1898.

S. J. Turnovsky, *Macroeconomic Analysis and Stablization Policy*, Cambridge, 1977.

K. Wicksell, *Geldzins und Güterpreise*, Jena, 1898. *Interest and Prices*, London, 1936.

———, *Föreläsningar i nationalekonomi, II*, Lund, 1906. *Lectures on Political Economy, II*, London, 1935.

A. Yarranton, *England's Improvement by Sea and Land. To Outdo the Dutch without Fighting. To Pay Debts without Moneys. To Set at Work all the Poor of England with the Growth of Our Own Lands . . .* , London, 1677; quoted from P. E. Dove, *Account of Andrew Yarranton*, Edinburgh, 1854.

Part II
The Short Run

4

Keynesian Short-Run Statics: One or Two Equilibrating Variables

Inflation, in 1936, seemed far from being a danger. —Hicks (1974:61)

On fiscal policy, Keynes expressed himself informally (1929, 1933). But his formal model (1936) had no fiscal policy in it. Here he tried to show the impotence of monetary policy: at a low rate of interest the demand for money was so sensitive to the rate of interest and investment demand so insensitive to it that the rate of interest could play no role as an equilibrating variable. If so, why not leave it out of the model? Working out a Keynesian theory of fiscal policy, Hansen (1941, 1951) did so as a first approximation and used physical output as his sole equilibrating variable. We shall do the same in the second section of the chapter but not in the third.

Any model of fiscal policy must deal with at least three magnitudes: physical government purchase of goods and services, the fiscal deficit, and the tax rate. All three cannot be parameters at the same time, or government could decide to buy all it cared for at zero or low tax rates, yet run a fiscal surplus. A choice will have to be made. The government can fix two of the three magnitudes as parameters and let the economy determine the third as a variable. Which two? There are three different ways in which two elements can be selected from three. That gives us three alternative priority patterns: either the government fixes government demand and the tax rate and lets the economy determine what the fiscal deficit will be, or the government fixes government demand and fiscal deficit and lets the economy determine the necessary tax rate, or, finally, the government fixes fiscal deficit and tax rate and lets the economy determine how much the government can afford to buy.

We adopt the last priority pattern—in harmony with our choice of the money and bond supplies as policy instruments to be made in chapters 5, 6, 8, and 9.

I. Notation

1. Variables

$C \equiv$ physical consumption
$D \equiv$ demand for money

$G \equiv$ physical government purchase of goods and services
$I \equiv$ physical investment
$R \equiv$ tax revenue
$r \equiv$ rate of interest
$X \equiv$ physical output
$Y \equiv$ money national income
$y \equiv$ money disposable income

2. Parameters

$A \equiv$ autonomous consumption
$c \equiv$ marginal propensity to consume real disposable income
$d \equiv$ fiscal deficit
$M \equiv$ supply of money
$P \equiv$ price of goods and services
$T \equiv$ tax rate

The models will include no derivatives with respect to time; hence they are static.

II. One Equilibrating Variable

1. The Model

For the time being treat investment, insensitive to the rate of interest, as autonomous and leave out the rate of interest as a variable. Consider a one-good economy with firms, households, and government in it.

Ignore capital consumption allowances, subsidies, indirect business tax, and business transfer payments. Then national income defined as the aggregate earnings arising from current production equals the money value of physical output.

$$Y \equiv PX \tag{4.1}$$

Ignore undistributed earnings. Then all national income becomes personal income, and disposable income will equal national income minus government gross receipts plus government transfer payments to persons, subsidies, and interest paid by government. Or, ignoring what the government collects with one hand only to pay back with the other, disposable income simply equals national income minus government net receipts:

$$y \equiv Y - R \qquad (4.2)$$

Let consumption be a function of real disposable income:

$$C = A + cy/P \qquad (4.3)$$

where $0 < c < 1$.

In Western tradition, as developed from the English Magna Carta of 1215, the Swedish Magna Carta at Uppsala of 1319, and the American Revolution of 1776, taxes are collected according to statute, and statute defines tax base and tax rate. Typical modern tax bases are assets, income, final sales, or value added. As a good first approximation, let tax revenue be in proportion to money national income:

$$R = TY \qquad (4.4)$$

where $0 < T < 1$.

Ignore the government interest bill and define the fiscal deficit as the money value of government purchase of goods and services minus government net receipts:

$$d \equiv GP - R \qquad (4.5)$$

Goods-market equilibrium requires the supply of goods to equal the demand for them:

$$X = C + I + G \qquad (4.6)$$

2. Solutions

To solve for our sole equilibrating variable, physical output X, insert 4.1 through 4.5 into 4.6 and find

$$X = \frac{A + I + d/P}{(1 - c)(1 - T)} \qquad (4.7)$$

To see how physical output depends on the fiscal deficit, take the derivative

$$\frac{\partial X}{\partial d} = \frac{1}{(1 - c)\,(1 - T)P} \tag{4.8}$$

Under the assumptions made about the parameters c and T, 4.8 is always positive: A larger deficit will generate a larger physical output!

To see how physical output depends on the tax rate, take the derivative

$$\frac{\partial X}{\partial T} = \frac{X}{1 - T} \tag{4.9}$$

where X stands for the output solution 4.7 above. Under the third priority pattern, the tax rate T is a parameter assumed to lie between zero and one. Consequently, the derivative 4.9 must have the same sign as output X; hence, if according to 4.7 X happens to be positive, the derivative 4.9 will be positive. The higher the tax rate, the higher the output. Is this surprising? Not when we remember that to keep the fiscal deficit d constant, government demand G must always increase by the same amount as tax revenue. And 215 years ago, James Steuart (1767:272) observed that taxation amounts to taking income away from households whose marginal propensity to spend it may fall short of unity, and transferring it to government whose marginal propensity to spend it must equal unity. In his own words Steuart expressed the positivity of 4.9:

> taxes promote industry; not in consequence of their being raised upon individuals, but in consequence of their being expended by the state; that is, by increasing demand and circulation.

Given the fiscal deficit d and the tax rate T, how much can the government afford to buy? Insert 4.1 and 4.4 into 4.5 and find

$$G = d/P + TX \tag{4.10}$$

To see how physical government purchase depends on the fiscal deficit, take the derivative

$$\frac{\partial G}{\partial d} = \frac{1 - c(1 - T)}{(1 - c)\,(1 - T)P} \tag{4.11}$$

Under the assumptions made about the parameters c and T, 4.11 is always positive. A larger deficit will permit a larger physical government purchase!

To see how physical government purchase depends on the tax rate, take the derivative

$$\frac{\partial G}{\partial T} = \frac{X}{1 - T} \qquad (4.12)$$

where again X stands for the output solution 4.7 above. Like 4.9, and for the same reason, the derivative 4.12 must have the same sign as output X; hence if according to 4.7 X happens to be positive, the derivative 4.12 will be positive. The higher the tax rate, the more the government can afford to buy. Is this surprising? Not when we remember that to keep the fiscal deficit d constant, government demand G must always increase by the same amount as tax revenue, and we just saw that the higher the tax rate the higher the physical output, hence the higher the tax revenue.

3. The Balanced-Budget Multiplier

Keynesians chose to consider physical government purchase G a parameter and the tax rate T a variable. Early Keynesians like Gelting (1941), Haavelmo (1945), and Samuelson (1948) found a balanced-budget multiplier equaling unity as the derivative of their single equilibrating variable, physical output X, with respect to their parameter G—assuming T to vary and keep the budget balanced.

Our choice is the opposite one. We consider physical government purchase G a variable and the tax rate T a parameter. But we can easily find our counterpart to the balanced-budget multiplier. Change our tax rate T by the differential dT, write the differentials $dX \equiv (\partial X/\partial T)dT$ and $dG \equiv (\partial G/\partial T)$ dT, divide the former by the latter, insert 4.9 and 4.12 and find

$$\frac{dX}{dG} \equiv \frac{\partial X/\partial T}{\partial G/\partial T} = 1 \qquad (4.13)$$

So here is a multiplier equaling unity. But notice that it holds under *any fixed* fiscal deficit. The balanced budget is the special case of a fixed deficit equaling zero. Nowhere did the literature seem to notice that the balanced-budget multiplier was derived under the unnecessarily narrow assumption of a balanced budget.

4. Crowding-Out Impossible

Until now all solutions and multipliers were found under the assumption of an autonomous physical investment I. Being autonomous, physical investment had no give in it and could not possibly be crowded out. Because our system had only one equilibrating variable—that is, physical output—the adjustment of saving to autonomous deficit and investment had to be brought about by adjustment of physical output alone. This is an extreme and very special case. Could there be an additional equilibrating variable?

III. Two Equilibrating Variables

1. The Rate of Interest As an Additional Equilibrating Variable

Realizing that the demand for money may be less sensitive and investment demand more sensitive to the rate of interest than Keynes had imagined, Hansen (1953:165) liked to think of the Keynesian system as having the rate of interest as a second equilibrating variable: "The rate of interest and the national income are together mutually determined by [the consumption function; the marginal efficiency of investment schedule; the liquidity preference schedule], together with the quantity of money."

Including the rate of interest as an equilibrating variable immediately raises the question: Which rate of interest, the nominal or the real one? Keynes knew, of course, but did not appreciate Fisher's distinction (1896) between a nominal and a real rate of interest. Keynes (1936:222–229) did consider "own rates" of interest, such as a wheat rate of interest or a copper rate of interest, and discussed their carrying-cost and liquidity aspects. He discussed Fisher's aspect of such own rates but remained unconvinced (1936:142–143). Happily he and Hansen (1949) begged the question by simply ignoring inflation. In that case the nominal and the real rate of interest will coincide, and one may invoke the celebrated *IS-LM* diagram. Had there been inflation one would have encountered the difficulty that the *IS* curve is a function of the real rate of interest, whereas the *LM* curve is a function of the nominal one. An *IS-LM* diagram has the single rate of interest r plotted on the vertical axis and physical output X on the horizontal one. The upper left corner of figure 4–1 shows the *IS* and *LM* curves.

The *IS* curve is the locus of all combinations of interest rate and output in which the goods market is in equilibrium: $X = C + I + G$. Because investment I is now sensitive to the rate of interest and is lower when the rate of interest is higher, equilibrium output will be low at a high rate of interest and high at a low one. The *IS* curve is negatively sloped.

The *LM* curve is the locus of all combinations of interest rate and output in which the money market is in equilibrium. Call the supply of money M and the demand for it D, then $M = D$. Because the demand for money is now sensitive to the rate of interest and is lower when the rate of interest is higher, a given money supply can transact a larger output at a high rate of interest than at a low one: the *LM* curve is positively sloped.

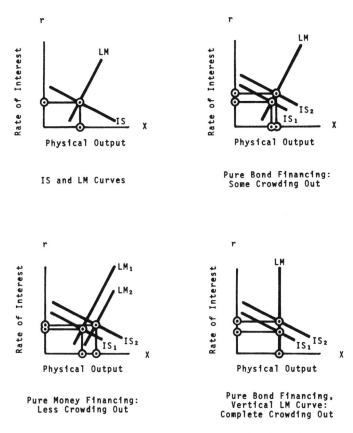

Figure 4–1. *IS-LM* Analysis of Deficit Financing

Keynes himself first saw the *IS-LM* diagram in 1937 and liked it [Patinkin (1976:100)], but not enough: it could have helped him understand his own system, but he refused the help.

2. Interest and Money: Keynes Misunderstood His Own System

Keynes always believed that his one and only rate of interest equilibrated the supply of and demand for money but never savings and investment. It was, as Patinkin (1976:99) puts it, a basic tenet of Keynes's theory "that savings and investment determined the level of income and *not* the rate of interest. . . . "

Such tidy compartmentalization misunderstands the nature of a system of simultaneous equations. Normally all variables are determined by all equations. The Keynesian system is no exception—as our *IS-LM* diagram shows. But Keynes's tradition was Marshallian partial equilibrium, not Walrasian general equilibrium.

Let us now apply the *IS-LM* diagram to fiscal policy.

3. Interest Rate and Fiscal Policy: Bond and Money Financing

Once the rate of interest is introduced as an additional equilibrating variable, the choice between alternative methods of financing a budget deficit becomes crucial. Let us consider pure bond and pure money financing in turn.

Let government expand its demand G but fail to raise taxes accordingly. Pure bond financing of the resulting government deficit means that the government issues interest-bearing claims on itself called bonds and sells them to households and firms. The money supply is not affected, and the *LM* curve stays put. The economy must still economize with the same quantity of money. But the expanded government demand has pushed the *IS* curve to the right. At a given rate of interest, the aggregate demand $C + I + G$ is up.

An *IS* curve pushed to the right will intersect an unchanged *LM* curve in a point whose abscissa and ordinate are both higher than before. The upper right corner of figure 4–1 shows this result. Output is up to satisfy the new government demand. The rate of interest is up. One effect of that is to discourage private investment—to some extent government is being satisfied at the expense of private investment, which is a weak case of crowding out. Another effect is to induce households and firms to hold less cash, so the larger output may be transacted.

Pure money financing of the government deficit means that the government issues noninterest-bearing claims on itself called money. The money supply is up, and the *LM* curve is now being pushed to the right—thus modifying the increase in the rate of interest and the resulting crowding out, as shown in the lower left corner of figure 4–1.

Alternatively we may define a strong sense of crowding out as zero sensitivity of physical output to a bond-financed government deficit. For such zero sensitivity to result, what would the *LM* curve have to be like? If an *IS* curve pushed to the right must intersect an *LM* curve in a point whose abscissa remains the same as before, the *LM* curve must stay put and be vertical. Such a case is shown in the lower right corner of figure 4–1. A vertical *LM* curve must mean that the demand for money is insensitive to the rate of interest: no rise in the latter will induce households and firms to hold less cash. No rise in the rate of interest will release any money to transact a larger output. Such complete insensitivity of the demand for money to the rate of interest was accepted by early monetarism [Friedman (1959)] but later abandoned [Friedman (1966, 1972)] and was an extreme and very special case—as extreme and as special as the Keynesian twin assumptions of a complete sensitivity of the demand for money and a complete insensitivity of the demand for investment to the rate of interest.

Finally, let us consider yet another possible equilibrating variable.

4. Price As an Additional Equilibrating Variable

If the demand for money were infinitely sensitive to the rate of interest and investment not sensitive to it at all, the rate of interest could play no role as an equilibrating variable, and Keynesian involuntary unemployment could occur. But could price play a role? To Patinkin (1956), price rather than the rate of interest offered itself as an additional equilibrating variable.

In a static Keynesian model let price and the money wage rate be flexible and responding to excess demand or supply. Let there be excess supply in the form of unemployment. As a result, let price and the money wage rate fall in the same proportion, so the real wage rate and labor supply is unaffected. The declining price will be raising the real value of money balances—the more so the farther price declines. Price will keep declining until the real-balance effect has become powerful enough to stimulate demand enough to restore full employment. The stimulus is the result of adding real wealth as an argument in the consumption function and will play its role even when the rate of interest can play no role. In Haberler's judgment (1952:241), such a real-balance effect "removes the narrow remaining base of . . . static competitive underemployment equilibrium"— and may, in that sense, be seen as a modern rehabilitation of Say's Law.

Generally, Keynesians have been reluctant to unfreeze price. In the cores of their fiscal-policy models neither Blinder-Solow (1974) nor Tobin-Buiter (1976) unfroze it. However, both went beyond Hansen's *IS-LM* analysis in another respect. Like Patinkin they added real wealth as an argument in the consumption function and, for good measure, in the demand-for-money function as well.

Unfreezing price within a static framework, as Patinkin did, will not illuminate inflation. What we need is a dynamic framework. Chapters 5 and 6 will provide one.

References

A. S. Blinder and R. M. Solow, "Analytical Foundations of Fiscal Policy," *The Economics of Public Finance* (Brookings), Washington, D.C., 1974.

I. Fisher, "Appreciation and Interest," *Publications of the American Economic Association*, Aug. 1896, *11*, 331–442.

M. Friedman, "The Demand for Money: Some Theoretical and Empirical Results," *J. Polit. Econ.*, Aug. 1959, *67*, 327–351.

——, "Interest Rates and the Demand for Money," *J. Law Econ.*, Oct. 1966, *9*, 71–85.

——, "Comments on the Critics," *J. Polit. Econ.*, Sep.-Oct. 1972, *80*, 906–950.

J. Gelting, "Nogle bemaerkninger om finansieringen af offentlig virksomhed," *Nationaløkonomisk Tidsskrift*, 1941, *79*, 293–299.

T. Haavelmo, "Multiplier Effects of a Balanced Budget," *Econometrica*, Oct. 1945, *13*, 311–318.

G. Haberler, "The Pigou Effect Once More," *J. Polit. Econ.*, June 1952, *60*, 240–246.

A. H. Hansen, *Fiscal Policy and Business Cycles*, New York, 1941.

——, *Monetary Theory and Fiscal Policy*, New York, 1949.

——, *Business Cycles and National Income*, New York, 1951.

——, *A Guide to Keynes*, New York, 1953.

J. Hicks, *The Crisis in Keynesian Economics*, Oxford, 1974.

J. M. Keynes, *Can Lloyd George Do It?*, London, 1929.

——, *The Means to Prosperity*, London, 1933.

——, *The General Theory of Employment, Interest and Money*, London, 1936.

D. Patinkin, *Money, Interest, and Prices*, Evanston, Ill., and White Plains, N.Y., 1956.

——, "Keynes' Monetary Thought: A Study of Its Development," *Hist. Polit. Econ.*, Spring 1976, *8*, 1–150.

P. Samuelson, "The Simple Mathematics of Income Determination," *Income, Employment and Public Policy, Essays in Honor of Alvin H. Hansen*, New York, 1948, 133–155.

J. Steuart, *An Inquiry into the Principles of Political Economy*, London, 1767, 1796.

J. Tobin and W. Buiter, "Long-Run Effects of Fiscal and Monetary Policy on Aggregate Demand," J. L. Stein (ed.), *Monetarism. Studies in Monetary Economics 1*, Amsterdam, 1976.

5 Short-Run Semidynamics: Government and Four Equilibrating Variables—A Nonaccommodating Fiscal Policy

We have defined "equilibrium" to be a situation with a balanced budget. This definition is appropriate to a static model. . . .
—Blinder-Solow (1974:49)

Appropriately in a static model, Blinder-Solow (1974:47) ignored price-level effects. The purpose of the present chapter is to revisit the balanced budget and see it in a less restrictive setting permitting inflation.

So we must unfreeze price. But it wouldn't do merely to move price P from our list of parameters to our list of variables. A static system would then tell us how high price would be. It is quite a different thing to tell how rapidly price is changing—which is what inflation is all about. So our new equilibrating variable should be the rate of inflation $g_P \equiv (dP/dt)/P$.

Any model admitting inflation as an equilibrating variable will, first, be inherently dynamic and, second, have two additional equilibrating variables: the nominal rate of interest r and the real rate of interest ρ. Our fourth equilibrating variable will be physical output X.

Our dynamics will be short-run semidynamics in the sense that we will not attempt to trace the effect of investment on physical capital stock, use a production function relating the flow of physical output to physical capital stock, or optimize the latter.

I. Notation

1. Variables

$C \equiv$ physical consumption
$D \equiv$ demand for money
$G \equiv$ physical government purchase of goods and services
$g_v \equiv$ proportionate rate of growth of variable v
$I \equiv$ physical net investment
$P \equiv$ price of goods and services

$\Pi \equiv$ price of bonds
$R \equiv$ tax revenue
$r \equiv$ nominal rate of interest
$\rho \equiv$ real rate of interest
$X \equiv$ physical output
$Y \equiv$ money national income
$y \equiv$ money disposable income

2. Parameters

$A \equiv$ autonomous consumption
$B \equiv$ autonomous net investment
$b \equiv$ marginal inducement to invest
$c \equiv$ marginal propensity to consume real disposable income
$f \equiv$ marginal inducement to hold money
$g_v \equiv$ proportionate rate of growth of parameter v
$H \equiv$ rate of inflation at zero excess capacity
$h \equiv$ sensitivity of rate of inflation to excess capacity
$i \equiv$ interest payment per annum per government bond
$J \equiv$ autonomous demand for money
$j \equiv$ marginal propensity to hold transaction money
$M \equiv$ supply of money
$Q \equiv$ physical quantity of government bonds outstanding
$T \equiv$ tax rate
$X_{\max} \equiv$ physical capacity

The model will include derivatives with respect to time t; hence it is dynamic.

II. The Model

Define the proportionate rate of growth of a magnitude v as

$$g_v \equiv \frac{dv}{dt}\frac{1}{v} \tag{5.1}$$

Consider a one-good economy with firms, households, and government. Ignore capital consumption allowances, subsidies, indirect business tax, and business transfer payments. Then national income, defined as the aggregate earnings arising from current production, equals net national product defined as the net market value of physical output:

$$Y \equiv PX \tag{5.2}$$

Expecting its suppliers to be forever raising their prices and labor to be forever raising its money wage rate, a firm will be compelled to contribute to inflation by raising its own price. Tempered by excess capacity, firms will try to keep abreast of inflation by raising their prices by

$$g_P = H - h(X_{\max} - X) \tag{5.3}$$

as shown in figure 5–1.

Once we allow for inflation, we must distinguish between two rates of interest: the nominal rate and the real rate. Define the real rate of interest as the nominal rate minus the rate of inflation:

$$\rho \equiv r - g_P \tag{5.4}$$

Let net investment be a function of the real rate of interest:

$$I = B - b\rho \tag{5.5}$$

as shown in figure 5–2.

Ignore undistributed earnings. Then all national income becomes personal income, and disposable income will equal national income minus government gross receipts plus government transfer payments, subsidies,

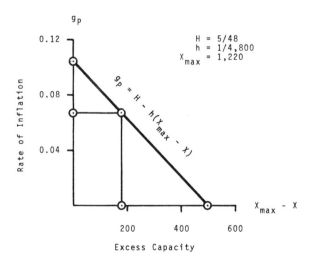

Figure 5–1. Inflation Tempered by Excess Capacity

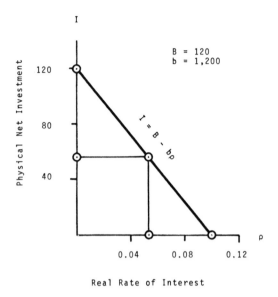

Figure 5-2. Net Investment as a Function of the Real Rate of Interest

and interest paid by government [Carson-Jaszi (1981)]. Or, ignoring what
the government collects with one hand only to pay back with the other,
disposable income simply equals national income minus government net
receipts. But in the present paper the bond supply Q is an important policy
instrument, and interest paid by government iQ should appear visibly rather
than being netted out. We define tax revenue R as government net receipts
before interest paid by government and write disposable income as

$$y \equiv Y + iQ - R \tag{5.6}$$

Let consumption be a function of real disposable income:

$$C = A + cy/P \tag{5.7}$$

where $0 < c < 1$ as shown in figure 5-3. Via 5.6, our consumption function
5.7 includes all real return on wealth—both the real return arising from
current production and included in Y/P and the real return not arising from
current production and included in iQ/P.

Let tax revenue be in proportion to money national income plus government interest bill:

$$R = T(Y + iQ) \tag{5.8}$$

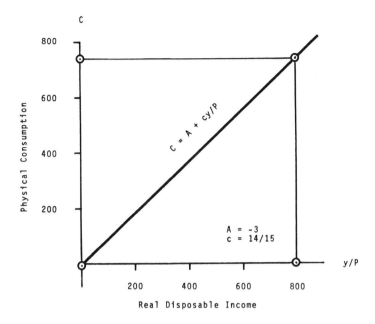

Figure 5–3.   Consumption as a Function of Real Disposable Income

where $0 < T < 1$, as shown in figure 5–4.

The dollar proceeds of a new bond issue equal price of bond times physical quantity of new bonds issued, or $\Pi dQ/dt$. Let the bonds be perpetuities whose market price is a capitalization of their future interest payments and let the nominal rate of interest r be stationary and used as a discount rate. The market price of a bond will then be in inverse proportion to the nominal rate of interest:

$$\Pi = i/r \tag{5.9}$$

The government budget constraint will then be

$$GP + iQ - R = \frac{dM}{dt} + \Pi \frac{dQ}{dt} \tag{5.10}$$

Let real demand for money be a function of the nominal rate of interest and the sum of real national income and real government interest bill:

$$D/P = J + j(Y + iQ)/P - fr \tag{5.11}$$

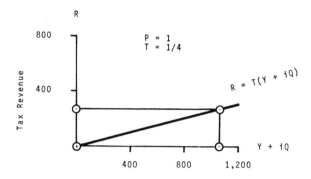

Figure 5–4.   Tax Revenue as a Function of Money National Income plus
Government Interest Bill

as shown in figure 5–5. Like our consumption function 5.7, our demand-for-
money function 5.11 includes all real return on wealth—both the real return
arising from current production and included in Y/P and the real return not
arising from current production and included in iQ/P.

Finally, let the system be in equilibrium. Goods-market equilibrium
requires the supply of goods to equal the demand for them:

$$X = C + I + G \qquad\qquad (5.12)$$

Money-market equilibrium requires the supply of money to equal the
demand for it:

$$M = D \qquad\qquad (5.13)$$

Figures 5–1 through 5–5 have been drawn using the following stylized
parameter values, not implausible for the United States in the 1970s,

$A = -3$
$B = 120$
$b = 1{,}200$
$c = 14/15$
$f = 300$
$H = 5/48$
$h = 1/4{,}800$
$iQ/P = 20$

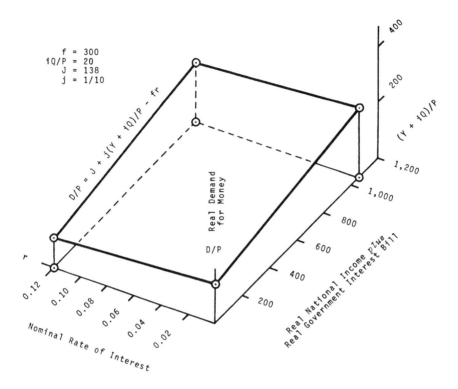

Figure 5–5. Real Demand for Money as a Function of the Nominal Rate of Interest and Real National Income plus Real Government Interest Bill

$$J = 138$$
$$j = 1/10$$
$$M/P = 208$$
$$T = 1/4$$
$$X_{\max} = 1,220$$

III. Solutions for Balanced-Budget Case

1. The Nominal Rate of Interest

Insert 5.2 and 5.8 into 5.6, 5.6 into 5.7, and write physical consumption as

$$C = A + c(1 - T)(X + iQ/P) \tag{5.14}$$

Insert 5.1, 5.2, 5.8, and 5.9 into 5.10 and write physical government purchase as

$$G = g_M M/P + (g_Q/r - 1)iQ/P + (X + iQ/P)T \qquad (5.15)$$

The division by r in the term g_Q/r is threatening to make our system nonlinear, but under a balanced budget the government deficit 5.10 is zero. Let a zero right-hand side of 5.10 be produced by letting our policy instruments—the rates of growth of the money and bond supplies—equal zero:

$$g_M = g_Q = 0 \qquad (5.16)$$

in which case 5.15 collapses into

$$G = -iQ/P + (X + iQ/P)T \qquad (5.17)$$

and the threatening nonlinearity of our system is averted by the disappearance of the term g_Q/r from equation 5.15.[1]

Insert the expressions 5.14 for C and 5.17 for G together with 5.5 into the goods-market equilibrium condition 5.12. Insert 5.3 and 5.4 into the result and find an IS curve:

$$r = \frac{A + B - (1 - c)(1 - T)iQ/P}{b}$$

$$+ \frac{(H - hX_{max})b - [(1 - c)(1 - T) - bh]X}{b} \qquad (5.18)$$

Insert 5.13 and 5.2 into 5.11 and find an LM curve:

$$X = \frac{M/P - J - ijQ/P + fr}{j} \qquad (5.19)$$

Insert the LM curve 5.19 into the IS curve 5.18 and find

$$r = q/u \qquad (5.20)$$

where

$$q \equiv [A + B - bhiQ/P + (H - hX_{max})b]j$$

$$- [(1 - c)(1 - T) - bh](M/P - J) \qquad (5.21)$$

$$u \equiv [(1 - c)(1 - T) - bh]f + bj \qquad (5.22)$$

2. Solutions for the Other Variables

Once we possess the solution 5.20 for the nominal rate of interest r, we may easily write solutions for our remaining three variables—all of which are linear functions of r. The *LM* curve 5.19 is a solution for physical output when r stands for 5.20. Inserting 5.19 into 5.3 and 5.4 will give us the solutions for the real rate of interest and the rate of inflation:

$$\rho = \frac{j - fh}{j} r - (H - hX_{\max}) - h \frac{M/P - J - ijQ/P}{j} \qquad (5.23)$$

$$g_P = \frac{fh}{j} r + H - hX_{\max} + h \frac{M/P - J - ijQ/P}{j} \qquad (5.24)$$

where r stands for 5.20. The government budget constraint 5.17 may be thought of as a solution for physical government purchase G, expressing it in terms of the variables r and X standing for 5.20 and 5.19, respectively.

Our system implies self-fulfilling expectations including inflationary ones; we used the same symbol for the expected and realized values of any variable, implying equality between the two. Is such equality always possible? Yes, if the system has a set of solutions. It has the set 5.20, 5.19, 5.23, and 5.24. Table 5–I shows policy instruments and solutions for all equilibrating variables, using the stylized parameter values listed at the end of section II.

Table 5–I
Consequences of a Nonaccommodating Fiscal Policy:
Initial Levels of Equilibrating Variables

Policy Instruments	
	Rates of Growth
Money Supply g_M	0
Bond Supply g_Q	0
Equilibrating Variables	
	Initial Levels
Nominal Interest Rate r	0.1200
Physical Output X	1040.0
Consumption C	739.0
Net Investment I	56.0
Government G	245.0
Real Interest Rate ρ	0.0533
Inflation Rate g_P	0.0667

IV. The Rates of Change of Solutions

1. Any Dynamics Left?

Turnovsky (1977:ix) characterized the presence of the derivatives with respect to time $dM/dt \equiv g_M M$ and $dQ/dt \equiv g_Q Q$ in the government budget constraint 5.10 as the "intrinsic dynamics" of fiscal policy. Such intrinsic dynamics disappeared from our model once we assumed—in 5.16—that the zero right-hand side of 5.10 was produced by a change in neither the money nor the bond supply.

If not intrinsic, some dynamics are left even under our balanced budget. Nowhere in our solutions do the money and bond supplies M and Q appear alone; they are always divided by price P. And P is indeed a function of time, for we have included its growth rate g_P among our equilibrating variables and found the solution 5.24 for it. Equation 5.16 may freeze the nominal money and bond supplies M and Q, but it cannot freeze the real ones M/P and Q/P. Let us now deal with such remaining dynamics.

2. The Total Derivative of Solutions with Respect to Time

All solutions 5.20, 5.19, 5.23, and 5.24 for our equilibrating variables contain the real money and bond supplies M/P and Q/P and nothing else which is a function of time. Consequently, solutions will be stationary if and only if M/P and Q/P are stationary, and they will be changing if and only if M/P and Q/P are changing. Let t represent time. The rates of change, if any, of our solutions will be described by their total derivatives with respect to time:

$$\frac{dr}{dt} \equiv \frac{\partial r}{\partial(M/P)} \frac{d(M/P)}{dt} + \frac{\partial r}{\partial(Q/P)} \frac{d(Q/P)}{dt} \tag{5.25}$$

$$\frac{dX}{dt} \equiv \frac{\partial X}{\partial(M/P)} \frac{d(M/P)}{dt} + \frac{\partial X}{\partial(Q/P)} \frac{d(Q/P)}{dt} \tag{5.26}$$

$$\frac{d\rho}{dt} \equiv \frac{\partial \rho}{\partial(M/P)} \frac{d(M/P)}{dt} + \frac{\partial \rho}{\partial(Q/P)} \frac{d(Q/P)}{dt} \tag{5.27}$$

$$\frac{dg_P}{dt} \equiv \frac{\partial g_P}{\partial(M/P)} \frac{d(M/P)}{dt} + \frac{\partial g_P}{\partial(Q/P)} \frac{d(Q/P)}{dt} \tag{5.28}$$

Let us now take all the derivatives present in the system 5.25 through 5.28. For compactness, let us write the results as the matrix multiplication shown in table 5–II. Partial differentiation of our solutions 5.20, 5.19, 5.23, and 5.24 will give us the two partial derivatives present in each of 5.25 through 5.28 constituting the first, second, third, and fourth rows, respectively of the center matrix in table 5–II. It follows from 5.1 that the time derivatives of M/P and Q/P can be written as $g_{(M/P)}M/P = (g_M - g_P)M/P$ and $g_{(Q/P)}Q/P = (g_Q - g_P)Q/P$, respectively, constituting, because $g_M = g_Q = 0$, the right-hand side column vector $(-g_P M/P, -g_P Q/P)$ of table 5–II. Under the stylized parameter values listed in section II, our matrix multiplication will give us the left-hand side column vector dr/dt, dX/dt, $d\rho/dt$, and dg_P/dt listed in table 5–III. Under such circumstances there is no way of keeping physical output from declining. Physical investment is declining, too. According to table 5–III the only variable displaying growth is the real rate of interest ρ. Inflation g_P is indeed subsiding.

V. Conclusions

Blinder-Solow (1974:49) defined "equilibrium" as a balanced budget and call their definition "appropriate to a static model of the type considered here." Their model could be static, because it did not include inflation.

Table 5–II
Rates of Change of Solutions for the Four Equilibrating Variables

$$
\begin{bmatrix} \dfrac{dr}{dt} \\[2em] \dfrac{dX}{dt} \\[2em] \dfrac{d\rho}{dt} \\[2em] \dfrac{dg_p}{dt} \end{bmatrix}
=
\begin{bmatrix} -\dfrac{(1-c)(1-T)-bh}{u} & -ij\dfrac{bh}{u} \\[2em] \dfrac{1}{j}\left[-\dfrac{(1-c)(1-T)-bh}{u}f+1\right] & i\left(-\dfrac{bh}{u}f-1\right) \\[2em] \dfrac{1}{j}\left[-(j-fh)\dfrac{(1-c)(1-T)-bh}{u}-h\right] & i\left[-(j-fh)\dfrac{bh}{u}+h\right] \\[2em] \dfrac{h}{j}\left[-\dfrac{(1-c)(1-T)-bh}{u}f+1\right] & hi\left(-\dfrac{bh}{u}f-1\right) \end{bmatrix}
\begin{bmatrix} -g_p M/P \\[2em] -g_p Q/P \end{bmatrix}
$$

Table 5–III
Consequences of a Nonaccommodating Fiscal Policy:
Initial Rates of Change of Equilibrating Variables

Policy Instruments	
	Rates of Growth
Money Supply g_M	0
Bond Supply g_Q	0

Equilibrating Variables	
	Initial Rates of Change
Nominal Interest Rate dr/dt	−0.0457
Physical Output dX/dt	−274.47
Real Interest Rate $d\rho/dt$	0.0115
Inflation Rate dg_P/dt	−0.0572

Because our model does include inflation, it is inherently dynamic. As a result, it can find the rates of change of its solutions for all four equilibrating variables. Under a balanced budget with inflation we have found the nominal rate of interest, physical output, and the rate of inflation to be declining over time but the real rate of interest to be growing. No equilibrating variable became stationary! The ultimate reason was, of course, that under inflation the frozen *nominal* money and bond supplies M and Q will always mean declining *real* money and bond supplies M/P and Q/P. Even our semidynamics, then, have made the Blinder-Solow definition inappropriate, and we must find a better one.

Note

1. But will be faced in the next chapter. As it will turn out, in a nonlinear system 5.16 will have to be thought of as a limit: $g_M = g_Q \to 0$.

References

A. S. Blinder and R. M. Solow, "Analytical Foundations of Fiscal Policy," *The Economics of Public Finance* (Brookings), Washington, D.C., 1974.

C. S. Carson and G. Jaszi, "The National Income and Products Accounts of the United States: An Overview," *Survey of Current Business*, Feb. 1981, 22–34.

S. J. Turnovsky, *Macroeconomic Analysis and Stabilization Policy*, Cambridge, 1977.

6

Short-Run Semidynamics: Government and Four Equilibrating Variables—An Accommodating Fiscal Policy

In the United States . . . two or three point-years of extra unemployment bring down the inertial core inflation by only one point.—Tobin (1981:38)

Let notation, variables, parameters, and equations 5.1 through 5.15 remain what they were in chapter 5, but define fiscal equilibrium as an accommodating rather than a balanced budget. Our precise definition of *accommodation* will be given by equation 6.14 below. With a nonbalanced budget, the budget constraint 5.10 is no longer zero. A nonzero government budget constraint is the key to three new properties of our model.

First, because it contains derivatives with respect to time, a nonzero government budget constraint is the key to the dynamics of our model.

Second, because it contains the price Π of bonds having—according to 5.9—the nominal rate of interest r in the denominator, a nonzero government budget constraint is the key to the nonlinearity of our model.

Third, a nonzero government budget constraint is the key to crowding out. Into the definition 5.6 insert the goods-market equilibrium condition 5.12 multiplied by P and with the definition 5.2 applied to it, rearrange, and write

$$y - CP = IP + GP + iQ - R$$

or, in English, in our closed economy savings equal investment plus government deficit. If and only if a budget is balanced—that is, $GP + iQ - R = 0$—will investment and saving be equal. Under a government deficit, investment falls short of saving and is in this sense being crowded out. Under a government surplus, investment exceeds saving—might one call it being crowded in? In short, a nonzero government budget constraint always displays crowding out or crowding in.

For the years 1977 through 1980 figure 1–5 recorded crowding out and crowding in in the United States, Japan, Germany, and France. Crowding out dominates the picture.

I. Solutions for Nonbalanced-Budget Case

1. *The Nominal Rate of Interest*

In the nonbalanced-budget case our system will be nonlinear, so we must now solve all over. In chapter 5 the balanced budget was first introduced by equation 5.16. Consequently we may still use equations 5.1 through 5.15. We insert 5.14 for consumption, 5.5 for investment, and 5.15 for government purchase into the goods-market equilibrium condition 5.12. Insert 5.3 and 5.4 into the result and find an *IS* curve:

$$r = \frac{A + B + g_M M/P + [g_Q/r - (1 - c)(1 - T)]iQ/P}{b}$$

$$+ \frac{(H - hX_{max})b - [(1 - c)(1 - T) - bh]X}{b} \tag{6.1}$$

Insert 5.13 and 5.2 into 5.11 and find an *LM* curve:

$$X = \frac{M/P - J - ijQ/P + fr}{j} \tag{6.2}$$

Insert the *LM* curve 6.2 into the *IS* curve 6.1 and find the quadratic equation in *r*:

$$r^2 - \frac{s}{u}r - \frac{g_Q ijQ/P}{u} = 0 \tag{6.3}$$

where

$$s \equiv [A + B + g_M M/P - bhiQ/P + (H - hX_{max})b]j$$

$$- [(1 - c)(1 - T) - bh](M/P - J) \tag{6.4}$$

$$u \equiv [(1 - c)(1 - T) - bh]f + bj \tag{6.5}$$

The roots of the quadratic equation 6.3 are the solutions for the nominal rate of interest

$$r = \frac{s}{2u} \pm \sqrt{\left(\frac{s}{2u}\right)^2 + \frac{g_Q ijQ/P}{u}} \tag{6.6}$$

We are no longer assuming $g_M = g_Q = 0$ but may still assume $g_M = g_Q$. Under such equalized policy instruments and under the stylized parameter values listed in section II of chapter 5, the roots 6.6 appear as the hyperbola shown in figure 6–1. For a balanced budget

$$g_M = g_Q = 0 \qquad\qquad (6.7)$$

the quadratic equation 6.3 would seem, on the face of it, to have the two roots $r = s/u$ and $r = 0$. But because 5.9 and 5.15 have terms in them in which r occurs as a denominator, our system is undefined for $r = 0$. All we can say, then, is that for $g_Q \to 0$, $\lim r = s/u$ and $\lim r = 0$.

2. Solutions for the Other Variables

Once we possess the solution 6.6 for the nominal rate of interest r, we may easily write solutions for our remaining three variables—all of which are

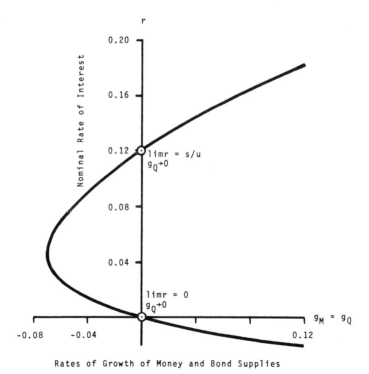

Figure 6–1. The Nominal Rate of Interest 6.6 as a Function of the Rates of Growth of the Money and Bond Supplies

linear functions of r. The LM curve 6.2 is a solution for physical output when r stands for 6.6. Inserting 6.2 into 5.3 and 5.4 will give us the solutions for the real rate of interest and the rate of inflation:

$$\rho = \frac{j - fh}{j} r - (H - hX_{\text{max}}) - h \frac{M/P - J - ijQ/P}{j} \quad (6.8)$$

$$g_P = \frac{fh}{j} r + H - hX_{\text{max}} + h \frac{M/P - J - ijQ/P}{j} \quad (6.9)$$

where r stands for 6.6. The government budget constraint 5.15 may be thought of as a solution for physical government purchase G, expressing it in terms of, first, the policy instruments g_M and g_Q and, second, the variables r and X standing for 6.6 and 6.2, respectively.

Again our system implies self-fulfilling expectations including inflationary ones; we used the same symbol for the expected and realized values of any variable, implying equality between the two. Is such equality always possible? Yes, if the system has a set of solutions. It has the set 6.2, 6.6, 6.8, and 6.9.

II. The Rates of Change of Solutions

All solutions 6.2, 6.6, 6.8, and 6.9 for our equilibrating variables contain the real money and bond supplies M/P and Q/P and nothing else which is a function of time. Consequently, solutions will be stationary if and only if M/P and Q/P are stationary, and they will be changing if and only if M/P and Q/P are changing. Let t represent time. The rates of change, if any, of our solutions will be described by their total derivatives with respect to time:

$$\frac{dr}{dt} \equiv \frac{\partial r}{\partial(M/P)} \frac{d(M/P)}{dt} + \frac{\partial r}{\partial(Q/P)} \frac{d(Q/P)}{dt} \quad (6.10)$$

$$\frac{dX}{dt} \equiv \frac{\partial X}{\partial(M/P)} \frac{d(M/P)}{dt} + \frac{\partial X}{\partial(Q/P)} \frac{d(Q/P)}{dt} \quad (6.11)$$

$$\frac{d\rho}{dt} \equiv \frac{\partial \rho}{\partial(M/P)} \frac{d(M/P)}{dt} + \frac{\partial \rho}{\partial(Q/P)} \frac{d(Q/P)}{dt} \quad (6.12)$$

$$\frac{dg_P}{dt} \equiv \frac{\partial g_P}{\partial(M/P)} \frac{d(M/P)}{dt} + \frac{\partial g_P}{\partial(Q/P)} \frac{d(Q/P)}{dt} \quad (6.13)$$

Let us take all the derivatives present in the system 6.10 through 6.13. For compactness let us write the results as the matrix multiplication shown in table 6–I. Implicit partial differentiation of the quadratic equation 6.3 with respect to M/P and Q/P will give us the two partial derivatives present in 6.10, constituting the first row of the center matrix of table 6–I. Partial differentiation of our solutions 6.2, 6.8, and 6.9 will then easily give us the two partial derivatives present in each of 6.11 through 6.13 constituting the second, third, and fourth rows, respectively of the center matrix of table 6–I. It follows from 5.1 that the time derivatives of M/P and Q/P can be written as $g_{(M/P)}M/P = (g_M - g_P)M/P$ and $g_{(Q/P)}Q/P = (g_Q - g_P)Q/P$, respectively, constituting the right-hand side column vector of table 6–I.

Now let our matrix multiplication collapse into a special case.

III. Fiscal Equilibrium

1. What Is an Accommodating Fiscal Policy?

Define an accommodating fiscal policy as one in which the growth rates of the money and bond supplies are equal and in turn equal to the growth rate of price P:

$$g_M = g_Q = g_P \tag{6.14}$$

Table 6–I
Rates of Change of Solutions for the Four Equilibrating Variables

$$
\begin{bmatrix} \dfrac{dr}{dt} \\[6pt] \dfrac{dX}{dt} \\[6pt] \dfrac{dp}{dt} \\[6pt] \dfrac{dg_p}{dt} \end{bmatrix}
=
\begin{bmatrix}
\dfrac{g_M j\ [(1\ c)(1\ T)\ bh]}{2ru-s}-r & ij\dfrac{g_Q-bh_i}{2ru-s} \\[12pt]
\dfrac{1}{j}\{\dfrac{g_M j-[(1-c)(1-T)-bh]}{2ru-s}-fr+1\} & i(\dfrac{g_Q-bhr}{2ru-s}-f-1) \\[12pt]
\dfrac{1}{j}\{(j-fh)\dfrac{g_M j-[(1-c)(1-T)-bh]}{2ru-s}-r-h\} & i[(j-fh)\dfrac{g_Q-bhr}{2ru-s}+h] \\[12pt]
\dfrac{h}{j}\{\dfrac{g_M j-[(1-c)(1-T)-bh]}{2ru-s}-fr+1\} & hi(\dfrac{g_Q-bhr}{2ru-s}-f-1)
\end{bmatrix}
\begin{bmatrix} (g_M-g_p)M/P \\[12pt] (g_Q-g_p)Q/P \end{bmatrix}
$$

In that case the right-hand side column vector of table 6–I collapses into a null vector. As a result

$$\frac{dr}{dt} = \frac{dX}{dt} = \frac{d\rho}{dt} = \frac{dg_P}{dt} = 0 \qquad (6.15)$$

or, in English, the nominal rate of interest, physical output, the real rate of interest, and the rate of inflation are all stationary, thus validating the assumption of a stationary nominal rate of interest underlying 5.9. Consequently, fiscal accommodation defined by 6.14 is an equilibrium in the sense, first, that all motion has come to an end and, second, that expectations are self-fulfilling.

2. The Algebra of Fiscal Accommodation

Fiscal accommodation defined by 6.14 may be an equilibrium, but does it exist? Are there values of our policy instruments g_M and g_Q obeying 6.14? To see if there are, first define two abbreviations:

$$q \equiv s - g_M jM/P$$

$$z \equiv H - hX_{\max} + h\,\frac{M/P - J - ijQ/P}{j}$$

Then insert 6.14 into 6.3 and 6.4, thus replacing g_Q and g_M, respectively, by g_P. Our solution 6.9 can now be inserted for g_P, enabling us to write 6.3 as the quadratic in r alone:

$$(u - fhM/P)r^2 - (q + jzM/P + fhiQ/P)r - ijzQ/P = 0 \quad (6.16)$$

Inserting the roots of 6.16 into 6.9 and 6.9 into 6.14, we find the values of $g_M = g_Q = g_P$ compatible with an accommodating fiscal policy. Under the stylized parameter values listed in section II of chapter 5, 6.16 has two real roots: $r = 0.0020$ and $g_M = g_Q = g_P = -0.0071$ for a surplus and $r = 0.1741$ and $g_M = g_Q = g_P = 0.1005$ for a deficit.[1] Table 6–II lists the economic consequences of such accommodating fiscal policies. Are those consequences meaningful to us and, if so, are they acceptable to the policymaker?

To us both roots are meaningful. No equilibrating variable is negative except the one whose negativity is meaningful—that is, the inflation rate $g_P = -0.0071$.

Table 6–II
Consequences of an Accommodating Fiscal Policy

	Surplus, Deflation	*Deficit, Inflation*
Policy Instruments	Rates of Growth	
Money Supply g_M	−0.0071	0.1005
Bond Supply g_Q	−0.0071	0.1005
Equilibrating Variables	Equilibrium Levels	
Nominal Interest Rate r	0.0020	0.1741
Physical Output X	686.1	1202.2
Consumption C	491.3	852.5
Net Investment I	109.1	31.7
Government G	85.8	318.0
Real Interest Rate ρ	0.0091	0.0736
Inflation Rate g_P	−0.0071	0.1005

To the policymaker, the first root $g_M = g_Q = g_P = -0.0071$—although meaningful—may be unacceptable. He may like the crowding in. The fiscal surplus, tantamount to positive public saving, makes investment exceed private saving. He may also like the negative inflation rate. But physical output— although sustainable—is 686.1 or merely 56 percent of capacity. That may seem too high a price to pay for a negative inflation rate.

A geometrical view of the two roots of 6.16 will now be helpful.

3. The Geometry of Fiscal Accommodation

The roots 6.6 appeared as the hyperbola of figure 6–1 showing the nominal rate of interest r as a function of the equalized policy instruments $g_M = g_Q$. Our linear equation 6.9 would appear as a positively sloped line showing the rate of inflation g_P as a function of the nominal rate of interest r.

In figure 6–2 we superimpose the line upon the hyperbola. The points, if any, in which the condition 6.14 would hold would appear as intersection points between the hyperbola and the line. For the stylized parameter values listed in section II of chapter 5 there are two intersection points, one with the lower, the other with the upper branch of the hyperbola.

The lower root 6.6 is generated by the minus sign preceding the square root of 6.6 or, geometrically, the one located on the lower branch of the hyperbola in figure 6–2. This branch intersects the positively sloped line representing 6.9 in a point whose coordinates are $g_M = g_Q = g_P = -0.0071$ and $r = 0.0020$—found when we solved our quadratic 6.16. It follows from the negative abscissa that this equilibrium is a surplus-deflation equilibrium. Here, both elements of the right-hand column vector of table 6–I are zero. All motion has come to an end.

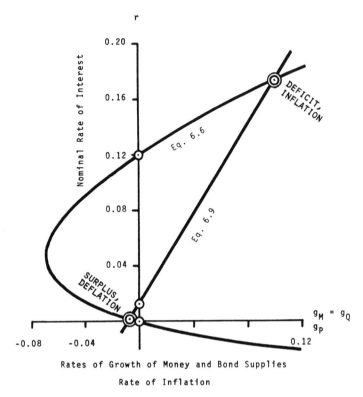

Figure 6–2. The Surplus-Deflation and Deficit-Inflation Points of an Accommodating Fiscal Policy

The higher root 6.6 is generated by the plus sign preceding the square root of 6.6 or, geometrically, the one located on the upper branch of the hyperbola in figure 6–2. This branch intersects the positively sloped line representing 6.9 in a point whose coordinates are $g_M = g_Q = g_P = 0.1005$ and $r = 0.1741$—found when we solved our quadratic 6.16. It follows from the positive abscissa that this equilibrium is a deficit-inflation equilibrium. Again, both elements of the right-hand column vector of table 6–I are zero. All motion has come to an end.

In either equilibrium, then, all motion has come to an end. But to the right and left of the equilibria there will be motion. The real money and bond supplies M/P and Q/P occur in both the hyperbola 6.6 and the line 6.9, consequently both will be moving. Let us see how.

4. An Expansionary Fiscal Policy

Define a nonaccommodating expansionary fiscal policy as one replacing
6.14 $g_M = g_Q = g_P$ by the inequality

$$g_M = g_Q > g_P \qquad (6.17)$$

Such raised policy instruments g_M and g_Q will allow a larger budget
deficit, hence a larger physical government purchase G, than an accommodating policy would have done. An expansionary fiscal policy is found to the
immediate right of either fiscal-accommodation equilibrium in figure 6–2.

To the immediate right of our surplus-deflation equilibrium in figure
6–2, the nominal rate of interest r is generating, according to 6.9, a negative
rate of inflation g_P less—more negative—than $g_M = g_Q$. To the immediate
right of our deficit-inflation equilibrium, the nominal rate of interest r
is generating, according to 6.9, a positive rate of inflation g_P less than
$g_M = g_Q$.

Consequently, to the right of either equilibrium $g_M - g_P > 0$ and
$g_Q - g_P > 0$. In that case, table 6–I will produce $dX/dt > 0$ and $dg_P/dt > 0$.
Physical output X and the rate of inflation g_P are both growing. As a result,
for as long as the high, supraequilibrium levels of g_M and g_Q are rigidly
adhered to by the policymaker, the rate of inflation g_P will keep moving up
toward the values $g_M = g_Q$ rigidly adhered to, thus tending to restore 6.14,
the definition of fiscal-accommodation equilibrium. The new equilibrium
has permanently higher physical output X and rate of inflation g_P than the
old equilibrium.

5. A Contractionary Fiscal Policy

Define a nonaccommodating contractionary fiscal policy as one replacing
6.14 $g_M = g_Q = g_P$ by the inequality

$$g_M = g_Q < g_P \qquad (6.18)$$

Such lowered policy instruments g_M and g_Q will allow a smaller budget
deficit, hence a smaller physical government purchase G, than an accommodating policy would have done. A contractionary fiscal policy is found to
the immediate left of either fiscal-accommodation equilibrium in figure 6–2.

To the immediate left of our surplus-deflation equilibrium in figure 6–2
the nominal rate of interest r is generating, according to 6.9, a negative rate

of inflation g_P greater—less negative—than $g_M = g_Q$. To the immediate left of our deficit-inflation equilibrium the nominal rate of interest r is generating, according to 6.9, a positive rate of inflation g_P greater than $g_M = g_Q$.

Consequently, to the left of either equilibrium $g_M - g_P < 0$ and $g_Q - g_P < 0$. In that case table 6-I will produce $dX/dt < 0$ and $dg_P/dt < 0$. Physical output X and the rate of inflation g_P are both declining. As a result, for as long as the low, subequilibrium levels of g_M and g_Q are rigidly adhered to by the policymaker, the rate of inflation g_P will keep moving down toward the values $g_M = g_Q$ rigidly adhered to, thus tending to restore 6.14, the definition of fiscal-accommodation equilibrium. The new equilibrium has permanently lower physical output X and rate of inflation g_P than the old equilibrium.

6. Stability of Equilibrium

We conclude that whenever the system is away from, either to the right or the left, of an equilibrium, whether the surplus-deflation equilibrium or the deficit-inflation equilibrium, equilibrium will eventually be restored. The system is stable!

Conventional macroeconomic stability discussion follows Blinder-Solow (1974:49), defines fiscal equilibrium as a balanced budget, and—in logical consequence—calls a fiscal policy stable if it generates responses that eventually restore budget balance. What is being restored in our own stability discussion is the absence of further motion in the four equilibrating variables. Neither of our two fiscal-accommodation equilibria ever displayed a budget balance—indeed, one of them was a surplus-deflation equilibrium, the other a deficit-inflation equilibrium!

7. A Trade-off Between Inflation and Excess Capacity?

If the policymaker is happy in one of our fiscal-accommodation equilibria, well and good. All he has to do is to fix his policy instruments at $g_M = g_Q = -0.0071$ or 0.1005 and adhere rigidly to such a value. If he is unhappy in any of the two equilibria, he will know what to do. An expansionary fiscal policy is available to the right of either equilibrium and a contractionary one to the left of it.

Those are his choices. He might wish to expand physical output and at the same time reduce the rate of inflation, but our model denies him that choice. Whichever way he tries to move, physical output and the rate of inflation are always moving in unison. Notice that the fourth row of table 6-I is h times the second row; consequently

$$\frac{dg_P}{dX} \equiv \frac{dg_P/dt}{dX/dt} = h \qquad (6.19)$$

What is h? According to equation 5.3, h is the absolute value of the slope of the Phillips curve, considered finite in the short run even by monetarists. Under the stylized parameter values listed in section II of chapter 5, $h = 1/4,800$. If so, anything that reduced the rate of inflation g_P by, say, 1/100 or one percentage point would reduce physical output by 48 or, which is the same thing, increase the rate of excess capacity $(X_{max} - X)/X_{max}$ from 0.01459 to 0.05393 or by about four percentage points. There is a roughly one-to-four impact split between inflation and excess capacity.

IV. Conclusions

We have built a short-run semidynamic model of a fiscal equilibrium defined as an accommodating rather than a balanced budget and using four equilibrating variables: the nominal rate of interest, physical output, the real rate of interest, and the rate of inflation. Solutions and their rates of change were found for all four equilibrating variables. The system was quadratic in the nominal rate of interest; hence it had two roots and two fiscal-accommodation equilibria, one displaying deflation and a fiscal surplus and the other displaying inflation and a fiscal deficit.

The rates of change of our solutions enabled us to examine the motion around these equilibria and the absence of it in the equilibria themselves, and to conclude that the equilibria were stable. Physical output and the rate of inflation were always moving in unison. Reducing the rate of inflation by one percentage point would always increase the rate of excess capacity by roughly four percentage points.

Part II, now coming to its end, confined itself to the short run and could thus afford to use a Phillips curve leaving no room for labor and labor's inflationary expectations. Part II used its dynamics sparingly and applied steady-state growth to price, not to physical output or to physical capital stock. Indeed, capital stock was never mentioned. We did not attempt to trace the effect of investment upon physical capital stock, use a production function relating the flow of physical output to physical capital stock, or optimize the latter. As a result, explicit discounting of future cash flows found no place in part II, and there was no occasion to examine how a discount rate might be affected by inflation and taxation. Part II took a narrow view of taxation and mentioned its income rather than its interest effect.

Part III will take a broader view and see all its variables in their natural habitat, a growing economy. For a fully dynamic setting we choose the neoclassical growth model. Let us begin by revisiting it.

Note

1. For the use of a root-finding CYBER routine I am grateful to the Computer Services Office of the University of Illinois and to Karen J. Brems and Hiroshi Miyashita.

References

A.S. Blinder and R.M. Solow, "Analytical Foundations of Fiscal Policy," *The Economics of Public Finance* (Brookings), Washington, D.C., 1974.
J. Tobin, "The Monetarist Counter-Revolution Today—An Appraisal," *Econ. J.*, March 1981, *91*, 29–42.

**Part III
The Long Run**

7

Long-Run Dynamics: The Neoclassical Growth Parable Revisited

The choice at the moment seems to be between exponential steady states and paths that depart ever further from steady states. Given this choice, the steady state seems the better approximation to the facts of economic growth.
—Solow in Burmeister-Dobell (1970:ix)

Our short-run semidynamics in chapters 5 and 6 made an attempt neither to trace the effect of investment on physical capital stock nor to use a production function relating the flow of physical output to physical capital stock. Doing such things are part of long-run dynamics, and for a quarter century we have possessed a simple and powerful model doing them—that is, Solow's neoclassical growth model (1956), modestly referred to (1970) as a "parable." In this model, a fully employed economy produces a single good from labor and an immortal capital stock of that good. A production function, not necessarily of Cobb-Douglas form, permits substitution between labor and capital stock. Capital stock is the result of accumulated savings under an autonomously given propensity to consume.

In fact, the neoclassical growth model is even older. Halfway through World War Two, Tinbergen (1942) had published it complete with econometric estimates of its parameters for four countries. But he had done it in German behind enemy lines, and it remained in hiding until Klaassen, Koyck, and Witteveen (1959) made it available in English.

Before applying it to anything, let us set out the simplest version of a neoclassical growth model, using a Cobb-Douglas production function, and let us then confront it with history.

I. Notation

1. Variables

$C \equiv$ physical consumption
$g_v \equiv$ proportionate rate of growth of variable v
$I \equiv$ physical investment
$\kappa \equiv$ physical marginal productivity of capital stock
$L \equiv$ labor employed
$P \equiv$ price of goods and services

$S \equiv$ physical capital stock
$W \equiv$ money wage bill
$w \equiv$ money wage rate
$X \equiv$ physical output
$Y \equiv$ money national income
$Z \equiv$ money profits bill

2. Parameters

$a \equiv$ multiplicative factor of production function
$\alpha, \beta \equiv$ exponents of production function
$c \equiv$ propensity to consume
$F \equiv$ available labor force
$g_v \equiv$ proportionate rate of growth of parameter v

The model will include derivatives with respect to time; hence it is dynamic. All parameters are stationary except a and F, whose growth rates are stationary.

II. The Model

Define the proportionate rate of growth of variable v as

$$g_v \equiv \frac{dv}{dt}\frac{1}{v} \tag{7.1}$$

Define investment as the derivative of capital stock with respect to time:

$$I \equiv \frac{dS}{dt} \tag{7.2}$$

Let entrepreneurs apply a Cobb-Douglas production function

$$X = aL^{\alpha}S^{\beta} \tag{7.3}$$

where $0 < \alpha < 1$; $0 < \beta < 1$; $\alpha + \beta = 1$; and $a > 0$.

Let profit maximization under pure competition equalize real wage rate and physical marginal productivity of labor:

$$\frac{w}{P} = \frac{\partial X}{\partial L} = \alpha \frac{X}{L} \tag{7.4}$$

Multiply by PL and write the wage bill

$$W \equiv wL = \alpha PX \qquad (7.5)$$

Define physical marginal productivity of capital stock, called by Solow (1956:80) "the commodity own-rate of interest," as

$$\kappa \equiv \frac{\partial X}{\partial S} = \beta \frac{X}{S} \qquad (7.6)$$

Multiply by PS and write the profits bill

$$Z \equiv \kappa PS = \beta PX \qquad (7.7)$$

Define national money income as the sum of wage and profits bills:

$$Y \equiv W + Z \qquad (7.8)$$

Let consumption be a fixed proportion c of output:

$$C = cX \qquad (7.9)$$

where $0 < c < 1$.

Assume the labor market to clear:

$$L = F \qquad (7.10)$$

Goods-market equilibrium requires the supply of goods to equal the demand for them:

$$X = C + I \qquad (7.11)$$

III. Convergence to Steady-State Growth

To solve the system, insert 7.10 into the production function 7.3, differentiate the latter with respect to time, and find

$$g_X = g_a + \alpha g_F + \beta g_S \qquad (7.12)$$

Here g_a and g_F are parameters but g_S is a variable. Use equations 7.9, 7.11, 7.1, and 7.2 in that order to express it as

$$g_S = (1 - c)X/S \qquad (7.13)$$

Differentiate equation 7.13 with respect to time, use 7.1 and 7.12, and express the proportionate rate of acceleration of physical capital stock as

$$g_{gS} = g_X - g_S = \alpha(g_a/\alpha + g_F - g_S) \qquad (7.14)$$

In equation 7.14 there are three possibilities: if $g_S > g_a/\alpha + g_F$, then $g_{gS} < 0$. If

$$g_S = g_a/\alpha + g_F \qquad (7.15)$$

then $g_{gS} = 0$. Finally, if $g_S < g_a/\alpha + g_F$, then $g_{gS} > 0$. Consequently, if greater than equation 7.15, g_S is falling; if equal to 7.15, g_S is stationary; and if less than 7.15, g_S is rising. Furthermore, g_S cannot alternate around 7.15, because differential equations trace continuous time paths, and as soon as a g_S-path touched 7.15 it would have to stay there. Finally, g_S cannot converge to anything else than 7.15; if it did, by letting enough time elapse we could make the left-hand side of 7.14 smaller than any arbitrarily assignable positive constant ε, however small, without the same being possible for the right-hand side. We conclude that g_S must either equal $g_a/\alpha + g_F$ from the outset or, if it does not, converge to that value.

Insert equation 7.15 into 7.12 and find the growth rate of physical output

$$g_X = g_S \qquad (7.16)$$

Differentiate 7.6 with respect to time, use 7.16, and find the growth rate of the physical marginal productivity of capital stock

$$g_\kappa = 0 \qquad (7.17)$$

Insert 7.10 into 7.4, differentiate the latter with respect to time, use 7.16 and 7.15, and find the rate of growth of the real wage rate

$$g_{w/P} \equiv g_w - g_P = g_a/\alpha \qquad (7.18)$$

Growth theory usually merely solves for steady-state equilibrium growth rates, not for levels. There is, however, one steady-state equilibrium level we should like to find. Divide the production function 7.3 first by L, then by S, and find

$$X/L = a(S/L)^\beta$$

$$X/S = a(L/S)^\alpha$$

Raise the latter equation to the power $-1/\alpha$, rearrange, insert into the former equation, insert the result into 7.4, and write the level of the real wage rate

$$w/P = \alpha a^{1/\alpha}(S/X)^{\beta/\alpha}$$

Rearrange 7.13 and insert it to find the solution for the level of the real wage rate in an economy with no government:

$$w/P = \alpha a^{1/\alpha}[(1 - c)/g_X]^{\beta/\alpha} \qquad (7.19)$$

which will indeed be growing at the rate 7.18 and in which g_X stands for 7.15 and 7.16. This result is interesting for two reasons.

First, here is something which does depend on the propensity to save $1 - c$. None of the steady-state equilibrium growth rates 7.15 through 7.18 did. An economy otherwise equal but with twice the propensity to save $1 - c$ will at any time have twice the real wage rate w/P.

Second, notice the absence of employment L from 7.19. In steady-state equilibrium growth, an economy otherwise equal but with twice the employment L will at any time have accumulated twice the physical capital stock S and be producing twice the physical output X. As a result, its capital coefficient S/X and with it its real wage rate w/P will be the same regardless of the level of employment L. In other words, the populous economy with twice the employment L will not display a lower physical marginal productivity of labor and a lower real wage rate. No Malthusian overpopulation here—land is ignored and physical capital stock will accumulate as needed!

Let us now confront our growth-rate solutions with historical reality.

IV. Five Properties Confronted with Historical Reality

1. Convergence to Steady-State Growth of Output

As long as the growth rates g_a and g_F of technology and labor force, respectively, remain stationary, then according to our solutions 7.15 and 7.16 physical output should converge to a rising straight line in a semilogarithmic time diagram. Does it? Figure 7-1 reproduces two diagrams by the U.S. Department of Commerce (1973:97) showing U.S. and West German real gross national products in the 1870–1970 period.

Between 1870 and 1969, the U.S. real gross national product was growing at an average annual rate of 0.037, and the first curve of figure 7-1 shows how. A kink is visible around 1910. The growth rate of the labor force

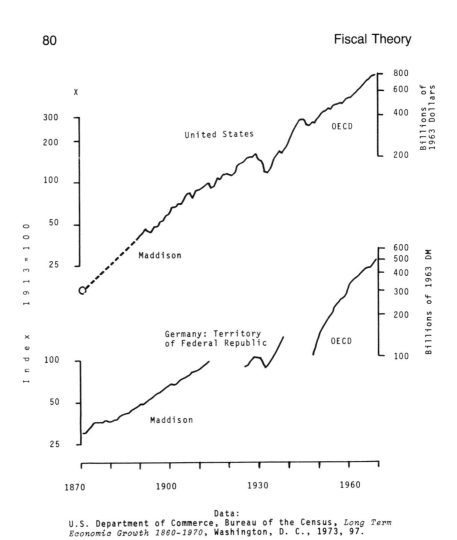

Data:
U.S. Department of Commerce, Bureau of the Census, *Long Term Economic Growth 1860-1970*, Washington, D. C., 1973, 97.

Figure 7–1.   Gross National Product X, United States and Germany, 1870–1970

is the net result of the birth, death, immigration, and participation rates, shown by the Department of Commerce (1973:31, 42). Whether measured in man-hours (p. 25) or in number of men (p. 29), a semilogarithmic U.S. labor force curve will display a conspicuous kink around 1910. That is the kink mirrored in the real gross national product curve of figure 7–1.

In the same period the West German real gross national product was growing at an average annual rate of 0.030. In 1945 the German economy lay in ruins. But in history's most perfect convergence, the 1948–1969 West

German curve in figure 7–1 swings back to an extrapolated 1870–1913 steady-state growth track!

2. Identical Steady-State Growth Rates of Output and Capital Stock but Not of Labor and Capital Stock

Early growth theory by Cassel (1923), Domar (1946), and Harrod (1948) used fixed input-output coefficients for both labor and capital. As a result, labor, capital, and output would all be growing at the same rate. In neoclassical growth, by contrast, according to our solution 7.15, capital stock should be growing more rapidly than labor but according to our solution 7.16 at the same rate as output. Does it?

Figure 7–2 displays findings by Kuznets (1971) for long periods and a number of industrial countries. The upper half shows the rate of growth of labor against that of capital. Cassel-Harrod-Domar theory, which requires the rates to be equal, is discredited. Neoclassical theory, allowing capital to be growing more rapidly than labor, is validated. The lower half of figure 7–2 shows the rate of growth of output against that of capital. If our solution 7.16 holds, all observations should lie on a 45° line. Do they? Practically on the 45° line are Canada (1891–1926), Norway (1879–1899), the United Kingdom (1925/29–1963), and the United States (1889–1929). But most countries show a tendency for output to grow slightly more rapidly than capital.

The most careful measurements of the growth of factor inputs so far are those by Christensen, Cummings, and Jorgenson (1980). Allowing for the decline of efficiency of a capital good with age, they measured capital stock as a weighted sum of past investments with geometrically declining efficiency weights. Such capital stock was then transformed into a flow of capital services. In addition to the mere quantity of capital stock, the flow reflected the quality of capital stock measured by its own rate of return. The own rate of return to capital was defined as the ratio of property compensation less depreciation to the value of capital stock. The quality thus defined was found to vary among the components of capital stock. If all components were growing at the same rate, the overall quality of capital stock would remain unchanged. Such was the case in only one of the nine countries studied—Germany. All other countries showed growing overall quality of capital stock. The rate of growth of real capital input was defined as the rate of growth of quality of capital stock plus the rate of growth of quantity of capital stock.

Labor input was measured similarly, except that the efficiency of labor was not assumed to be declining with age. The rate of growth of real labor

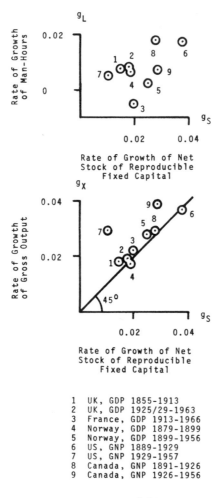

1   UK, GDP 1855-1913
2   UK, GDP 1925/29-1963
3   France, GDP 1913-1966
4   Norway, GDP 1879-1899
5   Norway, GDP 1899-1956
6   US, GNP 1889-1929
7   US, GNP 1929-1957
8   Canada, GNP 1891-1926
9   Canada, GNP 1926-1956

Data:
S. Kuznets, *Economic Growth of Nations, Total Output and Production
Structure*, Cambridge, Mass., 1971, 74-75.

Figure 7-2.   Growth Rates g_L, g_S, and g_X of Labor, Capital, and Output, Respectively, Five Countries, Late Nineteenth to Early
Twentieth Century

input was defined as the rate of growth of quality of hours worked plus the
rate of growth of hours worked.

Christensen, Cummings, and Jorgenson measured the growth of factor
inputs for nine countries from 1960 to 1973. Figure 7-3 displays their

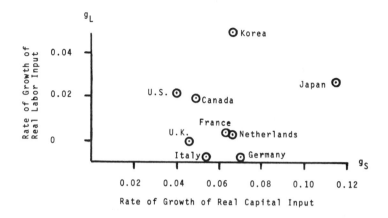

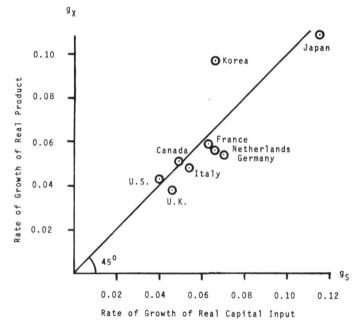

Data:
L. R. Christensen, D. Cummings, and D.W. Jorgenson, "Economic
Growth, 1947-73; An International Comparison," in J. W. Kendrick
and B. N. Vaccara (eds.), *New Developments in Productivity Measurement and Analysis*, Chicago and London 1980, 633.

Figure 7–3. Growth Rates g_L, g_S, and g_X of Labor, Capital, and Output,
Respectively, Nine Countries, 1960–1973

findings. First, the upper half of figure 7–3 shows the rate of growth of real labor input against the rate of growth of real capital input. Early growth theory, requiring the rates of growth of labor and capital to be equal, is once again discredited, and the neoclassical growth model, allowing capital to grow more rapidly than labor, is once again validated. Second, the lower half of figure 7–3 shows the rate of growth of real product against the rate of growth of real capital input. Neoclassical growth theory, requiring the two rates to be equal or at least converging to equal, is roughly true. Unlike the Kuznets measurements, the Christensen, Cummings, and Jorgenson measurements show a tendency for product to be growing slightly less rapidly than capital. More careful measurement of the quality of capital will classify as growth g_s of capital what would otherwise have been picked up by g_a.

Once the rates of growth of real labor input and real capital input have been measured and weighted by the distributive shares α and β, our equation 7.12 ascribes any remaining growth in real product to the growth rate g_a, sometimes referred to as technological progress. Christensen, Cummings, and Jorgenson prefer to call it the rate of growth of total factor productivity and estimate it as follows for the nine countries in the 1960–1973 period:

	g_a
Canada	0.018
France	0.030
Germany	0.030
Italy	0.031
Japan	0.045
Korea	0.041
Netherlands	0.026
United Kingdom	0.021
United States	0.013

3. Stationary Rate of Return to Capital

In an immortal capital stock, the physical marginal productivity κ of capital stock represents the rate of return to capital. If, as our solution 7.17 says, the physical marginal productivity κ of capital stock is growing at a zero rate, in a time diagram the rate of return to capital should appear as a horizontal line. Does it? Figure 7–4 displays findings by Kravis (1959) and Kendrick (1976). For the first half of the twentieth century Kravis calculated the ten-year moving averages shown in the upper half of figure 7–4. For the four decades from 1929 to 1969, Kendrick calculated the cycle averages shown in the lower half. Kravis and Kendrick differed with respect to concepts, method,

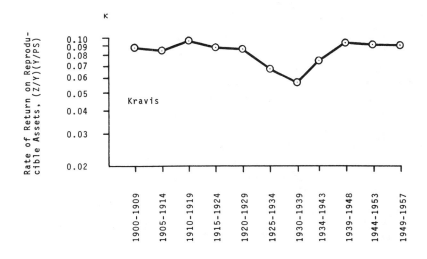

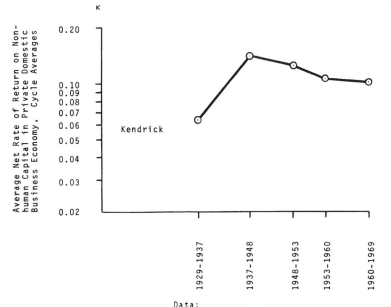

Data:

I. B. Kravis, "Relative Income Shares in Fact and Theory," *Amer. Econ. Rev.*, Dec. 1959, *49*, 938.

J. W. Kendrick assisted by Y. Lethem and J. Rowley, *The Formation and Stocks of Total Capital*, New York 1976, 124.

Figure 7–4.   Own Rate of Return on Capital κ, United States, 1900–1969

and scope. But they found roughly the same general level of return, the same trough of the Great Depression, and the same absence of any clear upward or downward trend.

Christensen, Cummings, and Jorgenson (1980) defined the nominal rate of return to capital as the ratio of property compensation less depreciation plus revaluation of assets to the value of capital stock. Corporate compensation was net of corporate income tax. Both corporate and noncorporate compensations were gross of personal income tax. The own rate of return to capital was then defined as the nominal rate less revaluation of assets. In other words, the own rate of return was defined as the ratio of property compensation less depreciation to the value of capital stock. For eight countries, time series for such own rates of return were offered—that is, from around 1950 to 1973. Figures 7–5 and 7–6 summarize the findings. Cyclical fluctuations dominate the picture in all countries. No clear trend is discernible except for Japan whose trend was distinctly upward.

4. Identical Steady-State Growth Rates of the Real Wage Rate and Labor Productivity

The real wage rate is w/P; hence its growth rate is $g_w - g_P$. According to solution 7.18 $g_w - g_P = g_a/\alpha$. Labor productivity is X/L; but according to equation 7.10 $L = F$. Hence the growth rate of labor productivity is $g_X - g_F$. Write our solutions 7.15 and 7.16 as $g_X - g_F = g_a/\alpha$. In other words, the growth rates of the real wage rate and labor productivity should be the same. Are they? Phelps Brown (1973) found the real wage rate and labor productivity to have been growing as follows:

	$g_{w/P}$	$g_{X/L}$
United States, 1890/99–1960	0.0208	0.0203
Germany, 1890/99–1960	0.0161	0.0151

In the United States and Germany the correspondence between $g_{w/P}$ and $g_{X/L}$ is striking.

5. Stationary Distributive Shares

Insert equations 7.5 and 7.7 into 7.8 and find $Y = PX$ and the distributive shares $W/Y = \alpha$ and $Z/Y = \beta$. So the distributive shares should remain stationary. Do they?

Denison (1974) measured labor's share in the United States from 1919 to 1968. He excluded government and income from investment abroad and

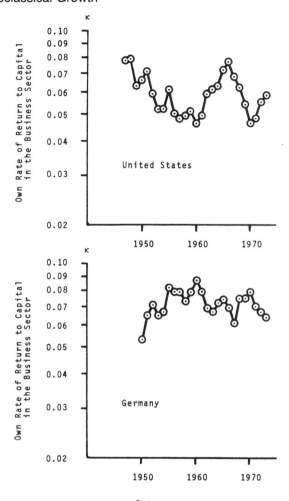

Data:
L. R. Christensen, D. Cummings, and D.W. Jorgenson, "Economic
Growth, 1947-73; An International Comparison," in J. W. Kendrick
and B. N. Vaccara (eds.), *New Developments in Productivity Measurement and Analysis*, Chicago and London 1980, 625.

Figure 7–5.   Own Rate of Return on Capital κ, United States, 1947–1973,
and Germany, 1950–1973

dwellings. Proprietors' income was imputed to labor and capital by first
assuming that proprietors were being paid the average wage rate of business
employees and earning the same rate of return on their assets as were
corporations. Then, if the sum of such imputed income items exceeded
actual proprietors' income (as it did in farming), all imputed income items

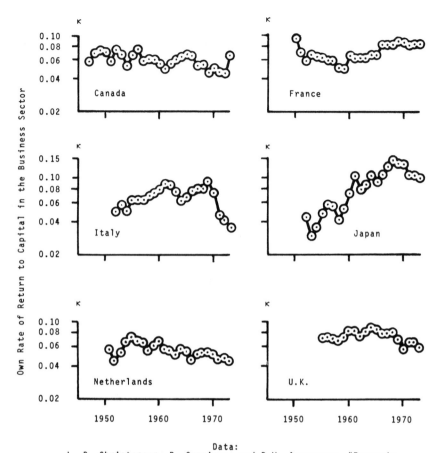

Own Rate of Return to Capital in the Business Sector

Data:
L. R. Christensen, D. Cummings, and D.W. Jorgenson, "Economic
Growth, 1947-73; An International Comparison," in J. W. Kendrick
and B. N. Vaccara (eds.), *New Developments in Productivity Measurement and Analysis,* Chicago and London 1980, 625.

Figure 7-6. Own Rate of Return on Capital κ, Six Other Countries,
1950s-1973

were reduced in the proportion of actual to imputed income. Left with
nonresidential business income, Denison calculated the U.S. shares displayed in the upper half of figure 7-7. They are practically stationary.

Equaling the exponents of the production function 7.3 the distributive
shares should be the same wherever Western technology is applied. Are
they? In his comparison of nine countries from 1960 to 1962, Denison (1967)
excluded income from the investment abroad and dwellings, as in his time-
series. But he did not exclude government. The inclusion of government

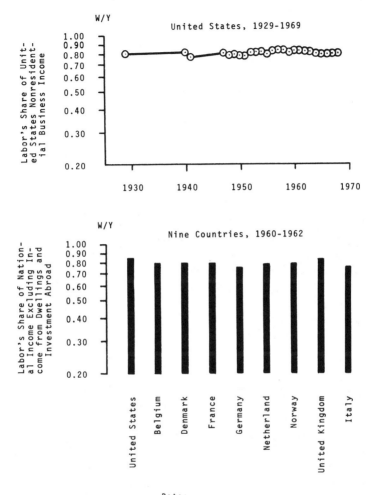

Data:

E. F. Denison, *Accounting for United States Economic Growth 1929-1969*, Washington, D. C., 1974, 260.

E. F. Denison, *Why Growth Rates Differ, Postwar Experience in Nine Western Countries*, Washington, D. C., 1967, 42.

Figure 7-7. Labor's Share W/Y, United States, 1929–1969, and Nine Countries, 1960–1962

would be harmless if "the importance of the compensation of general government employees in 1960–62 was about the same in Northwest Europe as a whole, in Italy, and in the United States." Less harmless was the lack of European data, which forced Denison to assume European proprietors' incomes to have the same labor's share as that calculated for the U.S. proprietors' income. With such hazards Denison calculated the shares displayed in the lower half of figure 7–7. They differ little among countries.

Christensen, Cummings, and Jorgenson (1980) included consumer durables in capital stock and an imputation for their services in total output. For 1970 their imputation amounted to one-tenth of the gross private domestic product—enough to make their distributive shares noncomparable to conventional ones.

6. Conclusions

The solutions of the neoclassical growth model possessed five important properties: (1) convergence to steady-state growth of output; (2) identical steady-state growth rates of output and capital stock but not of labor and capital stock; (3) stationary rate of return to capital; (4) identical steady-state growth rates of the real wage rate and labor productivity; and (5) stationary distributive shares. None of the five properties was found to be seriously at odds with historical reality.

7. What To Do Next

Macroeconomic theory has made little use of the neoclassical, or any other, growth model. Dealing with short-run unemployment, Keynesians obviously have had no use for a long-run full-employment model. The case of the monetarists is less obvious. Monetarists do invoke the long run and wish to exclude the rate of unemployment from their equilibrating variables. Yet they always ignore the neoclassical growth model. They shouldn't, as we shall see in chapter 8. The neoclassical growth model will require little modification to deliver most of Friedman's conclusions.

The neoclassical growth model is gaining ground as a macroeconomic tool. In his Radcliffe Lectures, Solow (1970:chapter 4) himself showed the way by adding a hybrid between money and government bonds. Later, Turnovsky (1977, 1978, and 1980) added government bonds, money, and taxes to a neoclassical growth model with a growing labor force but no technological progress. Brems (1980:chapter 6) added money, inflation, and unemployment. Stein (1982:chapter 5) sees monetary and fiscal policy in the framework of a growing economy. In chapter 9 we shall do the same and find Friedman's natural rate of unemployment to be not unique.

References

H. Brems, *Inflation, Interest, and Growth*, Lexington Books, D.C. Heath and Company, Lexington, Mass., 1980.

E. Burmeister and A.R. Dobell, *Mathematical Theories of Economic Growth*, New York and Toronto, 1970.

G. Cassel, *Theoretische Sozialökonomie*, Leipzig 1923, 51–52; *The Theory of Social Economy*, New York, 1924, 62–63.

L.R. Christensen, D. Cummings, and D.W. Jorgenson, "Economic Growth, 1947–73; An International Comparison," in J.W. Kendrick and B.N. Vaccara (eds.), *New Developments in Productivity Measurement and Analysis*, Chicago and London, 1980.

E.F. Denison, *Why Growth Rates Differ, Postwar Experience in Nine Western Countries*, Washington, D.C., 1967.

————, *Accounting for United States Economic Growth 1929–1969*, Washington, D.C., 1974.

E.D. Domar, "Capital Expansion, Rate of Growth, and Employment," *Econometrica*, Apr. 1946, *14*, 137–147.

R.F. Harrod, *Towards a Dynamic Economics*, London, 1948.

J.W. Kendrick assisted by Y. Lethem and J. Rowley, *The Formation and Stocks of Total Capital*, New York, 1976.

L.H. Klaassen, L.M. Koyck, and H.J. Witteveen (eds.), *Jan Tinbergen, Selected Papers*, Amsterdam, 1959.

I.B. Kravis, "Relative Income Shares in Fact and Theory," *Amer. Econ. Rev.*, Dec. 1959, *49*, 917–949.

S. Kuznets, *Economic Growth of Nations, Total Output and Production Structure*, Cambridge, Mass., 1971.

E.H. Phelps Brown, "Levels and Movements of Industrial Productivity and Real Wages Internationally Compared, 1860–1970," *Econ. J.*, Mar. 1973, *83*, 58–71.

R.M. Solow, "A Contribution to the Theory of Economic Growth," *Quart. J. Econ.*, Feb. 1956, *70*, 65–94.

————, *Growth Theory—An Exposition*, New York and Oxford, 1970.

J.L. Stein, *Monetarist, Keynesian, and New Classical Economics*, New York and London, 1982.

J. Tinbergen, "Zur Theorie der langfristigen Wirtschaftsentwicklung," *Weltw. Archiv*, May 1942, *55*, 511–549.

S.J. Turnovsky, *Macroeconomic Analysis and Stabilization Policy*, Cambridge, 1977.

————, "Macroeconomic Dynamics and Growth in a Monetary Economy," *J. Money, Credit, and Banking*, Feb. 1978, *10*, 1–26.

————, "Monetary and Fiscal Policy in a Long-Run Macroeconomic Model," *Econ. Record*, June 1980, *56*, 158–170.

U.S. Department of Commerce, Bureau of the Census, *Long Term Economic Growth 1860–1970*, Washington, D.C., 1973.

8 Monetarist Long-Run Dynamics: Three Equilibrating Variables

The monetary authority controls nominal quantities. . . . It cannot use its control over nominal quantities to peg a real quantity—the real rate of interest, the rate of unemployment. . . .   —Friedman (1968:11)

Monetarists wish to include the rate of inflation among their equilibrating variables. Any model admitting inflation as an equilibrating variable will immediately have two additional ones: the nominal and the real rate of interest. That distinction by Fisher (1896) is the strength of monetarists from Turgot (1769–1770) to Mundell (1971).

Monetarists wish to exclude the rate of unemployment from their equilibrating variables. "Monetary policy," says Friedman (1968:5), "cannot peg the rate of unemployment for more than very limited periods." A Friedman model, then, must dismiss and go beyond such limited periods and for that reason alone become a long-run model. But there is an additional reason. Using annual data, Friedman (1959) found real money holdings rather insensitive to current real income but more sensitive to permanent real income.

Friedman has always been reluctant to specify his own model. We hope to show that, with little modification, the neoclassical model of long-run growth will deliver most of his conclusions.[1] Chapter 7 restated that model, traced the effect of investment on physical capital stock, and used a production function relating the flow of physical output to physical capital stock, but did not optimize the latter. We should now like to optimize it.

Optimization of physical capital stock would involve maximization of present net worth. Present net worth of an asset is defined as its present gross worth minus its price of acquisition. Present gross worth is found by discounting the future cash flows generated by the asset, and the discount rate used is crucial. The discount rate used must reflect the cost of capital faced by the firm, and that cost is affected by taxation, as suggested by Feldstein (1976).

We must include taxation, then, but let it be as simple as possible. Let money national income be taxed once and at the uniform rate T. Let capital gains be tax-exempt. Let interest expense be tax-deductible. So if there is a market in which money may be placed or borrowed at the stationary nominal rate of interest r, if interest earnings are taxed at the rate T, and if interest expense is tax-deductible, money may be placed or borrowed at the aftertax rate $(1 - T)r$. That is the rate to be applied when discounting future cash flows, and we shall apply it. As a result, the tax rate T will appear in our expressions for the real rate of interest, desired capital stock, and desired investment.

I. Notation

1. Variables

$C \equiv$ physical consumption
$D \equiv$ desired holding of money
$G \equiv$ physical government purchase of goods and services
$g_v \equiv$ proportionate rate of growth of variable v
$I \equiv$ physical investment
$k \equiv$ present gross worth of another physical unit of capital stock
$\kappa \equiv$ physical marginal productivity of capital stock
$L \equiv$ labor employed
$n \equiv$ present net worth of another physical unit of capital stock
$P \equiv$ price of goods and services
$R \equiv$ tax revenue
$r \equiv$ before-tax nominal rate of interest
$\rho \equiv$ aftertax real rate of interest
$S \equiv$ physical capital stock
$w \equiv$ money wage rate
$X \equiv$ physical output
$Y \equiv$ money national income
$y \equiv$ money disposable income

2. Parameters

$a \equiv$ multiplicative factor of production function
$\alpha,\beta \equiv$ exponents of a production function
$c \equiv$ propensity to consume
$F \equiv$ available labor force
$g_v \equiv$ proportionate rate of growth of parameter v
$\lambda \equiv$ proportion employed of available labor force
$M \equiv$ supply of money
$m \equiv$ multiplicative factor of demand-for-money function
$\mu \equiv$ exponent of demand-for-money function
$T \equiv$ tax rate

The model will include derivatives with respect to time; hence it is dynamic. All parameters are stationary except a, F, and M, whose growth rates are stationary.

II. The Model

Define the proportionate rate of growth of variable v as

$$g_v \equiv \frac{dv}{dt} \frac{1}{v} \tag{8.1}$$

Define investment as the derivative of capital stock with respect to time:

$$I \equiv \frac{dS}{dt} \tag{8.2}$$

Monetarists have shown no interest in specifying a production function but may not object, we hope, to a Cobb-Douglas form

$$X = aL^\alpha S^\beta \tag{8.3}$$

where $0 < \alpha < 1$; $0 < \beta < 1$; $\alpha + \beta = 1$; and $a > 0$.

Let profit maximization under pure competition equalize real wage rate and physical marginal productivity of labor:

$$\frac{w}{P} = \frac{\partial X}{\partial L} = \alpha \frac{X}{L} \tag{8.4}$$

Rearrange 8.4 and write the neoclassical mark-up-pricing equation

$$P = \frac{wL}{\alpha X} \tag{8.5}$$

saying that neoclassical price P equals per-unit labor cost wL/X marked up in the proportion $1/\alpha$.

Define physical marginal productivity of capital stock as

$$\kappa \equiv \frac{\partial X}{\partial S} = \beta \frac{X}{S} \tag{8.6}$$

Let entrepreneurs be purely competitive; then price P of output is beyond their control. At time t, then, aftertax marginal value productivity of capital stock is $(1 - T)\kappa(t)P(t)$.

Let there be a market in which money may be placed or borrowed at the stationary nominal rate of interest r. Let interest earnings be taxed and interest expense be tax-deductible. Then money may be placed or borrowed at the aftertax rate $(1 - T)r$. Let that rate be applied when discounting future cash flows. As seen from the present time τ, then, aftertax marginal value productivity of capital stock is $(1 - T)\kappa(t)P(t)e^{-(1 - T)r(t - \tau)}$. Define present gross worth of another physical unit of capital stock as the present worth of all future aftertax marginal value productivities over its entire useful life:

$$k(\tau) \equiv \int_\tau^\infty (1 - T)\kappa(t)P(t)e^{-(1 - T)r(t - \tau)}dt \qquad (8.7)$$

Let entrepreneurs expect physical marginal productivity of capital stock to be growing at the stationary rate g_κ:

$$\kappa(t) = \kappa(\tau)e^{g_\kappa(t - \tau)}$$

and price of output to be growing at the stationary rate g_P:

$$P(t) = P(\tau)e^{g_P(t - \tau)}$$

Insert these into 8.7, define

$$\rho \equiv (1 - T)r - (g_\kappa + g_P) \qquad (8.8)$$

and write the integral 8.7 as

$$k(\tau) = \int_\tau^\infty (1 - T)\kappa(\tau)P(\tau)e^{-\rho(t - \tau)}dt$$

Neither $(1 - T)$, $\kappa(\tau)$, nor $P(\tau)$ is a function of t; hence they may be taken ouside the integral sign. Our g_κ, g_P, and r were all said to be stationary; hence the coefficient ρ of t is stationary, too. Assume $\rho > 0$. As a result find the integral to be

$$k = (1 - T)\kappa P/\rho \qquad (8.9)$$

Find present net worth of another physical unit of capital stock as its gross worth minus its price:

$$n \equiv k - P = [(1 - T)\kappa/\rho - 1]P$$

Desired capital stock is the size of stock for which the present net worth of another physical unit of capital stock equals zero, or

$$(1 - T)\kappa = \rho \qquad (8.10)$$

At first sight—incredibly!—it seems that taxation stimulates investment. Insert the definition 8.8 into the result 8.10, divide through by $1 - T$, and write it as

$$\kappa = r - (g_\kappa + g_P)/(1 - T) \qquad (8.8, 8.10)$$

Since $0 < T < 1$ and since therefore $(g_\kappa + g_P)/(1 - T) > g_\kappa + g_P$, then if nothing else were different the desired physical marginal productivity κ of capital stock would be lower with taxation than without. That, in turn, could be accomplished only by a desired capital stock and investment larger with taxation than without. Taxation stimulates investment! Something else, however, will be different—that is, the rates of interest, as we shall see once we have solved for them in section 8.IV.2.

Finally take equations 8.6 and 8.10 together and find desired capital stock

$$S = (1 - T)\beta X/\rho \qquad (8.11)$$

In accordance with the definition (8.2), differentiate desired capital stock 8.11 with respect to time, and write desired investment

$$I \equiv \frac{dS}{dt} = (1 - T)\beta g_X X/\rho \qquad (8.12)$$

If we think of 8.11 and 8.12 as being derived for an individual entrepreneur, then everything except X on their right hand sides is common to all entrepreneurs. Factor out all common factors, sum over all entrepreneurs, then X becomes national physical output, and 8.11 and 8.12 become national desired capital stock and investment, respectively.

For all their attention to crowding out, monetarists have shown little interest in deriving investment functions like 8.12. But let us take a closer look at 8.11 and 8.12 just the same. Both are in inverse proportion to ρ. What is ρ? In the definition 8.8 of ρ, let it be correctly foreseen that $g_\kappa = 0$—our steady-state growth and inflation model will indeed have the solutions 8.26 and 8.32, and historically the physical marginal productivity κ has displayed no secular trend, see section 7,IV,3. In that case ρ collapses into the aftertax real rate of interest.

Once priced according to 8.5, physical output becomes national income.

Let capital stock be immortal, so we may ignore capital consumption allowances and define national income as the money value of physical output

$$Y \equiv PX \tag{8.13}$$

Define money disposable income before capital gains as national income minus government net receipts:

$$y \equiv Y - R \tag{8.14}$$

Let real wealth in the neoclassical model consist of real money stock M/P and the physical capital stock S. Real capital gains on money stock are $-g_P M/P$ and on physical capital stock zero. Consequently real disposable income after capital gains is $(Y - R - g_P M)/P$, and let consumption be the fraction c of that:

$$C = c(Y - R - g_P M)/P \tag{8.15}$$

Let labor employed be the proportion λ of available labor force:

$$L = \lambda F \tag{8.16}$$

where $0 < \lambda < 1$. The difference $1 - \lambda$ is the "natural" rate of unemployment below which, according to Friedman (1968:8) excess demand for labor will push the real wage rate up, and above which excess supply will push it down. Friedman sees the employment fraction λ, then, as a long-run Walrasian equilibrium determined by the intersection of supply and demand curves invulnerable to monetary policy. Could they be vulnerable to policy other than monetary policy? They could well be. A minimum-wage statute can cut off the demand curve at the point at which the real minimum wage rate equals the physical marginal productivity of labor. As a result the employment fraction λ is down. Or an unemployment-compensation statute can shift the supply curve to the left by raising the rate of unemployment compensation or lengthen the maximum period of entitlement. As a result, the hardship of unemployment is reduced, the incentive to look for jobs is reduced, and again the employment fraction λ is down. Even a Walrasian long-run equilibrium thus amended by modern institutional arrangements would still generate an employment fraction λ to be considered a parameter by *monetary* policy.

Let tax revenue be in proportion to money national income:

$$R = TY \tag{8.17}$$

and let the government finance its deficit, if any, by issuing noninterest-bearing claims upon itself called money. The government budget constraint is then

$$GP - R = \frac{dM}{dt} \qquad (8.18)$$

Let the demand for money be a function of money national income and of the aftertax nominal rate of interest[2]:

$$D = mY[(1 - T)r]^{\mu} \qquad (8.19)$$

where $\mu < 0$ and $m > 0$.

Goods-market equilibrium requires the supply of goods to equal the demand for them:

$$X = C + I + G \qquad (8.20)$$

Money-market equilibrium requires the supply of money to equal the demand for it:

$$M = D \qquad (8.21)$$

We may now proceed to solving the system for the growth rates of its variables and for the level of its aftertax real rate of interest.

III. Steady-State Equilibrium Growth Solutions

1. Growth-Rate Solutions

By differentiating equations 8.1 through 8.21 with respect to time, the reader may convince himself that they are satisfied by the following steady-state growth solutions

$$g_C = g_X \qquad (8.22)$$

$$g_D = g_M \qquad (8.23)$$

$$g_G = g_X \qquad (8.24)$$

$$g_I = g_X \qquad (8.25)$$

$$g_\kappa = g_X - g_S \tag{8.26}$$

$$g_L = g_F \tag{8.27}$$

$$g_M = g_Y \tag{8.28}$$

$$g_R = g_Y \tag{8.29}$$

$$g_r = 0 \tag{8.30}$$

$$g_\rho = 0 \tag{8.31}$$

$$g_S = g_X \tag{8.32}$$

$$g_{w/P} = g_a/\alpha \tag{8.33}$$

$$g_X = g_a/\alpha + g_F \tag{8.34}$$

$$g_Y = g_P + g_X \tag{8.35}$$

$$g_y = g_Y \tag{8.36}$$

Our growth was steady-state growth because no right-hand side of our solutions 8.22 through 8.36 was a function of time.

2. Properties of Growth-Rate Solutions

Our growth-rate solutions neatly deliver Friedman's conclusions. First, no growth-rate solution for the nine real variables $C, G, I, \kappa, L, \rho, S, w/P$, and X has the rate of growth g_M of the money supply in it, directly or indirectly. Second, the growth-rate solutions for the five nominal variables D, P, R, Y, and y have the rate of growth g_M of the money supply in them, directly or indirectly. The growth-rate solution for the sixth nominal variable, r, does not (but its level does, as we shall see in section 8.IV). Third, the rate of growth g_M of the money supply may be thought of as a policy instrument used to control inflation: Take the growth-rate solutions 8.28 and 8.35 together, insert 8.34, and find

$$g_P = g_M - (g_a/\alpha + g_F)$$

or, in English, knowing the rate of technological progress g_a and the rate of growth of the labor force g_F and knowing the elasticity α of physical output with respect to labor, the monetary authorities may control the rate of inflation g_P by controlling the rate of growth g_M of the money supply. Do monetarists have a point? For nine countries whose monetary policies differed markedly between 1975 and 1980, Batten (1981) found a rather close correspondence between g_P and g_M, reproduced graphically in figure 8-1.

IV. Steady-State Equilibrium Level Solutions: The Rates of Interest

1. Interest and Money: Friedman

To Friedman (1968:11), the real rate of interest equilibrates savings and investment but never the supply of and the demand for money. The supply

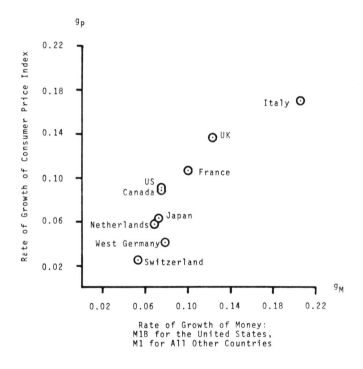

Data:
D. S. Batten, "Inflation: The Cost-Push Myth," *Federal Reserve Bank of St. Louis Review*, June/July 1981, *63*, 23, table 1.

Figure 8-1. Money Growth and Inflation in Major Industrial Nations, IV/1975–IV/1980.

of and the demand for money is equilibrated by the nominal rate of interest. Generating inflation and inflationary expectations, a larger money supply will raise, not lower, the nominal rate of interest. The contrast to Keynes is complete, but Friedman's neat compartmentalization may fare no better than did the Keynesian one. To see if it does, we must solve for the levels of the rates of interest.

2. The Aftertax Real Rate of Interest

In steady-state growth theory it is usually easier to solve for growth rates than for levels. Can we solve for our aftertax real rate of interest ρ? Insert the goods-market equilibrium condition 8.20 into the left-hand side of the investment function 8.12 and write the aftertax real rate of interest

$$\rho = \frac{(1 - T)\beta g_X X}{X - (C + G)}$$

Insert the definition 8.13 of national income and the tax function 8.17 into the consumption function 8.15 and the government budget constraint 8.18 and write physical consumption and government purchase, dividing by price P. Insert them into the denominator $X - (C + G)$. Finally divide both numerator and denominator by $(1 - T)X$, use 8.13 to write PX as Y, and write the aftertax real rate of interest

$$\rho = \beta g_X / A \tag{8.37}$$

where

$$A \equiv 1 - c - \frac{(g_M - c g_P)M/Y}{1 - T}$$

Do we find government and its policy instruments present here?

The first term of A is $1 - c$, the propensity to save real disposable income in an economy knowing neither government nor inflation. The presence of the second term of A is the consequence of government deficits and inflation. First, had the budget been balanced, $g_M = 0$, the first term of the coefficient of M/Y would not have been there. Being there and being preceded by a minus sign, it is telling us that some saving otherwise available to finance investment is now being channeled into financing a government deficit. Second, had there been no inflation, $g_P = 0$, households would have suffered no negative capital gains from it, and the second term $c g_P$ of the coefficient of M/Y would not have been there. Being there and being preceded by a double minus sign it is telling us that the negative capital gains resulting from inflation are reducing consumption—that is, augmenting saving.

Does A have a simple economic meaning, then? It has. Multiply both sides of 8.37 by $1 - T$, insert our investment function 8.12, find

$$(1 - T)A = I/X \qquad (8.12, 8.37)$$

and realize that $(1 - T)A$ is simply the fraction of output invested in an economy knowing government and inflation. Indeed government and its policy instruments are present in 8.37!

Equation 8.37 has both the real and the nominal rate of interest in it. In its aftertax form, the real rate of interest appears visibly on the left-hand side. In its aftertax form, the nominal rate of interest is hiding behind M/Y. Insert the money-market equilibrium condition 8.21 into the demand-for-money function 8.19; divide both sides by Y, and write

$$M/Y = m[(1 - T)r]^{\mu} \qquad (8.19, 8.21)$$

In steady-state growth equilibrium, the money supply will be growing in accordance with solution 8.28, i.e., at the same rate $g_M = g_Y$ as money national income. As a result, in such an equilibrium the money-income ratio M/Y, and with it the aftertax nominal rate of interest, will remain stationary.

It follows equally clearly from 8.19 and 8.21 that unless the stationary level of the money-income ratio M/Y differs from one such steady-state growth equilibrium to another, the aftertax nominal rate of interest $(1 - T)r$ cannot differ. Because $\mu < 0$, a low money-income ratio means a high aftertax nominal rate of interest, and a high money-income ratio means a low aftertax nominal rate of interest.

Finally, the definition 8.8 relates the aftertax nominal rate of interest to the aftertax real rate:

$$(1 - T)r \equiv \rho + g_\kappa + g_P \qquad (8.8)$$

Allowing for all this we should like to know if and how, according to 8.37, ρ depends on inflation and taxation.

3. Sensitivity of Aftertax Real Rate of Interest to Inflation

Let us compare a more inflationary steady-state equilibrium growth track having a higher $g_M = g_Y$ to a less inflationary track. Will the aftertax real rate of interest ρ differ between the two tracks? To see if it will, we must differentiate 8.37 with respect to the rate of inflation g_P.

To make sure that all interest rates are free to vary, we must leave the money-income ratio M/Y free to vary. We do that by inserting 8.8, 8.19, and 8.21 into 8.37 before the differentiation. But with those equations inserted into it, 8.37 will have the sum $\rho + g_\kappa + g_P$ raised to the power μ in it and will not permit an explicit solution for ρ. Implicit differentiation of 8.37, then, is our only way of establishing the sensitivity of ρ to g_P. Into A of 8.37 insert

$$M/Y = m(\rho + g_\kappa + g_P)^\mu \qquad (8.8), (8.19), (8.21)$$

$$g_M = g_Y = g_P + g_X \qquad (8.28), (8.35)$$

but consider neither β, c, g_κ, g_X, m, μ, nor T a function of the rate of inflation g_P. Then differentiate 8.37 with respect to g_P. Upon the result, use 8.8, 8.19, and 8.21 once again and write it as

$$\frac{\partial \rho}{\partial g_P} = -\beta g_X \frac{J - (1 - c)(1 - T)M/Y}{A^2(1 - T)^2 + \beta g_X J} \qquad (8.38)$$

where

$$J \equiv [(1 - c)g_P + g_X](-\mu M/Y)/r$$

Using the following values, not implausible for the United States in the late 1970s,

$A = 0.08404$
$\beta = 0.2$
$c = 0.91$
$g_\kappa = 0$
$g_P = 0.07$
$g_X = 0.02$
$M/Y = 0.17$
$\mu = -0.2$
$r = 0.1568$
$\rho = 0.0476$
$T = 0.25$

we find the sensitivity 8.38 of the aftertax real rate of interest to the rate of inflation to be 0.00578. So if the more inflationary growth track has a one percentage point higher rate of inflation g_P, it will have a 0.00578 percentage point higher aftertax real rate of interest ρ. According to 8.8, it will then have a 1.00578 percentage point higher aftertax nominal rate of interest $(1 - T)r$ and a 1.3410 percentage point higher before-tax nominal rate of interest r.

The sensitivity of the aftertax real rate of interest is small but magnifies itself into the sensitivity of both a nominal and a real variable. The nominal one is the before-tax nominal rate of interest, which is up by much more than the aftertax real rate is up and by a good bit more than the rate of inflation is up.

To see the second magnification we must go back to our equilibrium condition 8.10, saying that the physical marginal productivity κ must equal $\rho/(1 - T)$. Consequently, if the more inflationary growth track has a 0.00578 percentage point higher aftertax real rate of interest ρ, it must have a 0.00771 percentage point higher physical marginal productivity κ of capital stock.

4. Sensitivity of Aftertax Real Rate of Interest to Taxation

Next, let us compare a high-tax equilibrium growth track to a low-tax track having the same $g_M = g_Y$. Will the aftertax real rate of interest ρ differ between the two tracks? To see if it will, we must differentiate 8.37—again implicitly!—with respect to the tax rate T. Into A of 8.37 insert

$$M/Y = m(\rho + g_\kappa + g_P)^\mu \qquad (8.8), (8.19), (8.21)$$

$$g_M = g_Y = g_P + g_X \qquad (8.28), (8.35)$$

but consider neither β, c, g_κ, g_M, g_P, g_X, m, nor μ a function of the tax rate T. Then differentiate 8.37 with respect to T. Upon the result, use 8.8, 8.19, and 8.21 once again and write it as

$$\frac{\partial \rho}{\partial T} = \beta g_X \frac{[(1 - c)g_P + g_X]M/Y}{A^2(1 - T)^2 + \beta g_X J} \qquad (8.39)$$

where J was defined in 8.38. For the numerical values listed in section 8.IV.3, the sensitivity 8.39 of the aftertax real rate of interest to the tax rate is 0.00448. So if the high-tax growth track has a one percentage point higher tax rate T, it will have a 0.00448 percentage point higher aftertax real rate of interest ρ. According to 8.8, it will then have a 0.00448 percentage point higher aftertax nominal rate of interest $(1 - T)r$ and a 0.2180 percentage point higher before-tax nominal rate of interest r.

The sensitivity of the aftertax real rate of interest is small but again magnifies itself into the sensitivity of both a nominal and a real variable. The nominal one is the before-tax nominal rate of interest, which is up by much more than the aftertax real rate is up (and the rate of inflation is not even up at all).

To see the second magnification, we again go back to our equilibrium condition 8.10, saying that the physical marginal productivity κ must equal $\rho/(1 - T)$. Now the higher the taxation, the higher the ρ and the smaller the fraction $1 - T$. Consequently, if the high-tax growth track has a 0.00448 percentage point higher aftertax real rate of interest ρ, it must have a 0.09183 percentage point higher physical marginal productivity κ of capital stock. The latter is up by much more than the aftertax real rate of interest is up. As a result, the high-tax growth track must have a significantly lower desired capital stock and investment than the low-tax track. That effect might be called the Feldstein Effect (1976).

V. Nonsteady-State Growth: Crowding Out and Crowding In

1. Rate of Growth of Physical Capital Stock

Insert the definition 8.13 of national income and the tax function 8.17 into the consumption function 8.15 and the government budget constraint 8.18 and write physical consumption and government purchase, dividing by price P. Use 8.1 and 8.2 to write $I \equiv g_S S$, insert all that into the goods-market equilibrium condition 8.20, factor out $(1 - T)X$, use 8.13 to write PX as Y, and write the rate of growth of physical capital stock

$$g_S \equiv \frac{I}{S} = \frac{X - (C + G)}{S} = \frac{(1 - T)AX}{S} \tag{8.40}$$

where A was defined in 8.37. The key to our analysis of accommodating and nonaccommodating monetary-fiscal policies will be the rate of growth of that rate of growth—that is, the rate of acceleration of physical capital stock

$$g_{gS} = g_A + g_X - g_S \tag{8.41}$$

If there is a unique natural employment fraction λ—and in chapter 9 we shall doubt it—we may set $g_\lambda = 0$. In that case, insert 8.16 into the production function 8.3, differentiate with respect to time, and find

$$g_X = g_a + \alpha g_F + \beta g_S \tag{8.42}$$

Insert 8.42 into 8.41 and find the rate of acceleration of physical capital stock to be

$$g_{gS} = g_A + \alpha(g_a/\alpha + g_F - g_S) \tag{8.43}$$

Consider three alternative monetary-fiscal policies. The first allows everything to grow in accordance with our steady-state equilibrium-growth solutions 8.22 through 8.36 and will be called an accommodating monetary-fiscal policy.

The second monetary-fiscal policy allows the money supply M to be growing more rapidly than money national income Y. At a given tax rate such a policy will allow a larger budget deficit, hence a larger physical government purchase G, than an accommodating policy would have done and is therefore called expansionary.

The third monetary-fiscal policy allows the money supply M to grow less rapidly than money national income Y. At a given tax rate, such a policy will allow a smaller budget deficit, hence a smaller physical government purchase G, than an accommodating policy would have done and is therefore called contractionary.

2. An Accommodating Monetary-Fiscal Policy

Consider an economy finding itself in the steady-state equilibrium growth defined by solutions 8.22 through 8.36. Define an accommodating monetary-fiscal policy as one upholding solution 8.28:

$$g_M = g_Y \tag{8.28}$$

In the expression A as defined in 8.37, the ratio M/Y will then be stationary, and the expression A itself will be stationary, too:

$$g_A = 0 \tag{8.44}$$

In that case the rate of acceleration of physical capital stock 8.43 collapses into

$$g_{gS} = \alpha(g_a/\alpha + g_F - g_S) \tag{8.45}$$

Equation 8.45 has three possibilities: if $g_S > g_a/\alpha + g_F$, then $g_{gS} < 0$. If

$$g_S = g_a/\alpha + g_F \tag{8.46}$$

then $g_{gS} = 0$. Finally, if $g_S < g_a/\alpha + g_F$, then $g_{gS} > 0$. Consequently if greater than equation 8.46, g_S is falling; if equal to 8.46, g_S is stationary; and if less than 8.46, g_S is rising. Furthermore, g_S cannot alternate around 8.46, because differential equations trace continuous time paths, and as soon as a g_S-path touched 8.46 it would have to stay there. Finally, g_S cannot converge to anything else than 8.46; if it did, by letting enough time elapse we could make the left-hand side of 8.45 smaller than any arbitrarily assignable positive constant ε, however small, without the same being possible for the right-hand side. We conclude that g_S must either equal $g_a/\alpha + g_F$ from the outset or, if it does not, it must converge to that value.

Insert 8.46 into 8.42 and find the rate of growth of physical output

$$g_X = g_S$$

which was indeed our steady-state equilibrium-growth solution 8.32.

As we just saw, under an accommodating monetary-fiscal policy, the expression A as defined in 8.37 will remain stationary. As a result, the aftertax real rate of interest 8.37 will remain stationary, too, and there will be neither crowding out or crowding in.

3. An Expansionary Monetary-Fiscal Policy: Crowding Out

Define an expansionary monetary-fiscal policy as one replacing our solution 8.28 by the inequality

$$g_M > g_Y \tag{8.47}$$

The expression A as defined in 8.37 will be changing if and only if M/Y is changing. By the definition 8.47 M/Y is growing. For as long as it is, A will be declining:

$$g_A < 0$$

In that case the rate of acceleration of physical capital stock 8.43 will be

$$g_{gS} < \alpha(g_a/\alpha + g_F - g_S) \tag{8.48}$$

Under an accommodating monetary-fiscal policy g_{gS} was equal to $\alpha(g_a/\alpha + g_F - g_S)$, and hence would become zero when $g_S = g_a/\alpha + g_F$. Now g_{gS} is less than that; hence, it will still be negative once $g_S = g_a/\alpha + g_F$. But a negative g_{gS} means that g_S is still declining and will keep doing so as it approaches a level below $g_a/\alpha + g_F$. To summarize, under an expansionary monetary-fiscal policy, private physical capital stock S will eventually grow less rapidly than at the rate $g_a/\alpha + g_F$ and is in this sense being crowded out. The reason is easy to see.

As we just saw, under an expansionary monetary-fiscal policy the expression A as defined in 8.37 will decline. As a result, the aftertax real rate of interest 8.37 will grow—which explains the deceleration of physical capital stock and the crowding out just found.

4. A Contractionary Monetary-Fiscal Policy: Crowding-In

Define a contractionary monetary-fiscal policy as one replacing our solution 8.28 by the inequality

$$g_M < g_Y \qquad (8.49)$$

The expression A as defined in 8.37 will be changing if and only if M/Y is changing. By the definition 8.49 M/Y is declining. For as long as it is, A will be growing:

$$g_A > 0$$

In that case the rate of acceleration of physical capital stock 8.43 will be

$$g_{gS} > \alpha(g_a/\alpha + g_F - g_S) \qquad (8.50)$$

Under an accommodating monetary-fiscal policy, g_{gS} was equal to $\alpha(g_a/\alpha + g_F - g_S)$, hence would become zero when $g_S = g_a/\alpha + g_F$. Now g_{gS} is greater than that; hence, it will still be positive once $g_S = g_a/\alpha + g_F$. But a positive g_{gS} means that g_S is still growing and will keep doing so as it approaches a level above $g_a/\alpha + g_F$. To summarize, under a contractionary monetary-fiscal policy, private physical capital stock S will eventually grow more rapidly than at the rate $g_a/\alpha + g_F$. In this sense there is crowding in. The reason is easy to see.

As we just saw, under a contractionary monetary-fiscal policy the expression A as defined in 8.37 will grow. As a result, the aftertax real rate of interest 8.37 will decline—which explains the acceleration of physical capital stock and the crowding in just found.

Under the monetarist assumption of a "natural" rate of unemployment, our crowding-out and crowding-in results were clear-cut. In chapter 9 we shall drop that assumption and find modified crowding out and crowding in.

VI. Conclusions

1. Equilibrium Growth Rates versus Equilibrium Levels

Our growth-rate solutions 8.22 through 8.36 neatly delivered Friedman's conclusions. Did our level solutions do the same? Specifically, is it true that the monetary authority cannot use its control over nominal quantities to peg the real rate of interest?

Unlike chapter 7, this chapter has optimized physical capital stock. The optimization helped us find the equilibrium level of the aftertax real rate of interest. Comparing a more inflationary steady-state equilibrium growth track with a less inflationary track, we found the more inflationary one to have the higher aftertax real rate of interest. Did monetary policy make the difference? The more inflationary track had the higher rate of growth of the money supply. It had better, or it could not have sustained its higher inflation (the growth rate of physical output was supply-determined and could not differ between the two tracks). In that sense, inflation was indeed a consequence of monetary policy.

But our simple model was a model of a closed, bondless economy. Here, money could not come into existence in any other way than by financing a government budget deficit, and a government budget deficit could not be financed in any other way than by expanding the money supply. In that sense monetary and fiscal policy were inseparable; they were two aspects of the same thing—that is, deficit financing. We recognized that fact by always referring to "monetary-fiscal policy."

Can monetarists wash their hands of fiscal policy?[3] They cannot have it both ways. The monetarists gave us the crowding-out concept. In the monetarist view, an expansionary monetary-fiscal policy allowing a larger budget deficit will produce crowding out of physical investment. Vice versa, a contractionary monetary-fiscal policy allowing a smaller budget deficit should produce crowding in. Indeed, section 8.V found them doing just that. But how could crowding out and crowding in have occurred without growing and declining aftertax real rate of interest? Monetary-fiscal policy is indeed affecting it!

2. What to Do Next

We must give up our assumption of a bondless economy. A government budget deficit may be financed by expanding either the money or the bond supply, so we must use a full government budget constraint as we did in chapters 5 and 6.

Unlike chapters 5 and 6, the present chapter kept a record of physical capital stock, traced the effect of investment on physical capital stock, used a production function relating the flow of physical output to physical capital stock, and optimized the latter. On the other hand, neither the financial assets and liabilities of firms and households were recorded, nor were the budget constraints under which firms and households operate. A careful financial stock-flow bookkeeping might enable us to identify winners and losers in the inflation game.

So we have things to do, and we shall do them in Chapter 9.

Notes

1. Drud Hansen (1979) used a neoclassical growth model to simulate monetarism but—like Friedman himself—ignored taxation.

2. On the money-market side, monetarist tradition disaggregates more than we do and distinguishes among money, credit, and securities markets. On the goods-market side, monetarist tradition disaggregates less than we do and does not even distinguish between consumption and investment demand [Brunner-Meltzer (1976)]. A good recent survey of crowding out is Svindland (1980).

3. In his *Newsweek* column of July 12, 1982, Friedman said: "It is important to emphasize what monetarism is not. It has little to say about fiscal policy. . . ."

References

D. S. Batten, "Inflation: The Cost-Push Myth," *Federal Reserve Bank of St. Louis Review*, June/July 1981, *63*, 20–26.

K. Brunner and A. H. Meltzer, "An Aggregative Theory for a Closed Economy," J. L. Stein (ed.), *Monetarism. Studies in Monetary Economics 1*, Amsterdam, 1976.

J. Drud Hansen, *Den Friedmanske monetarisme*, Odense, Denmark, 1979.

M. Feldstein, "Inflation, Income Taxes, and the Rate of Interest: A Theoretical Analysis," *Amer. Econ. Rev.*, Dec. 1976, *66*, 809–820.

I. Fisher, "Appreciation and Interest," *Publications of the American Economic Association*, Aug. 1896, *11*, 331–442.

M. Friedman, "The Demand for Money: Some Theoretical and Empirical Results," *J. Polit. Econ.*, Aug. 1959, *67*, 327–351.

———, "Interest Rates and the Demand for Money," *J. Law Econ.*, Oct. 1966, *9*, 71–85.

———, "The Role of Monetary Policy," *Amer. Econ. Rev.*, Mar. 1968, *58*, 1–17.

R. A. Mundell, *Monetary Theory: Inflation, Interest, and Growth in the World Economy*, Pacific Palisades, 1971.

E. Svindland, "Staatsausgaben und ihre Finanzierung. Einige elementare Bemerkungen zu den Grundlagen der Crowding-Out Analyse," *Vierteljahreshefte zur Wirtschaftsforschung*, Heft 2, 1980, *49*, 148–179.

A. R. J. Turgot, "Réflexions sur la formation et la distribution des richnesses," *Ephémérides du citoyen*, Nov. 1769–Jan. 1770. *Reflections on the Formation and the Distribution of Riches*, New York, 1898.

9 Full Long-Run Dynamics: Government, Inflation, and Growth

For an exponentially growing economy it would be more natural to define fiscal equilibrium as a situation in which [the real money supply] and [the real bond supply] (and the stock of real capital) were growing at the same rate as [real income]. —Blinder-Solow (1974:49)

Let us explore Blinder-Solow's suggestion of a steady-state growth fiscal equilibrium, and let us do it within the framework of a neoclassical growth model [Solow (1956)] extended well beyond that in chapter 8.

Chapter 8 paid little attention to financial stock-flow relationships; neither financial assets and liabilities of firms and households were recorded, nor were the budget constraints under which firms and households operate. Only a government budget constraint was admitted and, even here, government bonds were left out. Careful financial stock-flow bookkeeping to be applied in this chapter will be used to introduce bonds and shares, see that the aftertax real rate of interest will be equal to the dividend yield, and see who are winners and losers in the inflation game.

Unlike chapter 8, this chapter will introduce a labor market and see the price-wage spiral as an interaction between a price and a wage equation. In two respects, monetarist doctrine will find no support. First, the rate of inflation will not normally be "accelerationist" but unique, stationary, and stable. Second, the "natural" rate of unemployment will not be unique. Its lack of uniqueness will help us modify simple monetarist notions about crowding out and crowding in.

I. Notation, Definitions, and Sectors

1. Variables

$C \equiv$ physical consumption
$D_b \equiv$ desired holding of bonds
$D_m \equiv$ desired holding of money
$D_s \equiv$ desired holding of shares
$\delta \equiv$ dividend payment per share
$G \equiv$ physical government purchase of goods and services
$g_v \equiv$ proportionate rate of growth of variable v

$I \equiv$ physical investment
$k \equiv$ present gross worth of another physical unit of capital stock
$\kappa \equiv$ physical marginal productivity of capital stock
$L \equiv$ labor employed
$\lambda \equiv$ proportion employed of available labor force
$N \equiv$ present net worth of entire physical capital stock
$n \equiv$ present net worth of another physical unit of capital stock
$P \equiv$ price of goods and services
$p \equiv$ coefficient in Phillips function representing inflationary potential
$\Pi_b \equiv$ price of a bond
$\Pi_s \equiv$ price of a share
$Q_s \equiv$ physical quantity of industry shares outstanding
$R \equiv$ tax revenue
$r \equiv$ before-tax nominal rate of interest
$\rho \equiv$ aftertax real rate of interest
$S \equiv$ physical capital stock
$V \equiv$ wealth
$W \equiv$ money wage bill
$w \equiv$ money wage rate
$X \equiv$ physical output
$Y \equiv$ money national income
$y \equiv$ money disposable income
$Z \equiv$ money profits bill

2. Parameters

$a \equiv$ multiplicative factor of production function
$\alpha, \beta \equiv$ exponents of a production function
$c \equiv$ propensity to consume
$F \equiv$ available labor force
$g_v \equiv$ proportionate rate of growth of parameter v
$i \equiv$ interest payment per bond
$M \equiv$ supply of money
$m \equiv$ multiplicative factor in demand-for-money function
$\mu \equiv$ exponent in demand-for-money function
$\pi \equiv$ exponent in Phillips function
$Q_b \equiv$ physical quantity of government bonds outstanding
$T \equiv$ tax rate
$\phi \equiv$ coefficient in Phillips function representing sensitivity to inflationary expectations

The model will include derivatives with respect to time. Hence, it is dynamic. All parameters are stationary except a, F, M, and Q_b whose growth rates are stationary.

3. Definitions

Define the proportionate rate of growth of variable v as

$$g_v \equiv \frac{dv}{dt} \frac{1}{v} \tag{9.1}$$

Define investment as the derivative of capital stock with respect to time:

$$I \equiv \frac{dS}{dt} \tag{9.2}$$

4. Three Sectors

Consider a one-good economy with three sectors—firms, households, and government—and use subscripts f, h, and g, respectively, to refer to them. Firms engage in production, hiring, pricing, and investment. Households engage in portfolio holding, consumption, work, and pricing the work. Government engages in purchasing goods and services, servicing the government debt, and collecting taxes.

Firms and governments normally have positive deficits and households normally negative deficits called saving. Deficits must be financed somehow. Let us follow Turnovsky (1977) and let firms finance theirs by supplying claims on themselves in the form of dividend-bearing shares, but let firms demand no claims. Let households save—and hence supply no claims on themselves—but demand claims on firms and government. Let government finance its deficit by supplying claims on itself in the form of noninterest-bearing money and interest-bearing bonds, but let government demand no claims.

For each sector, orderly bookkeeping requires recording all this in terms of stocks and flows. Let us meet this requirement by once again following Turnovsky. First, the balance sheet of a sector defines its wealth as assets minus liabilities, both valued at current market prices. Second, the budget constraint of a sector defines its deficit as its expenditure minus its revenue and says that a deficit on goods account must equal supply minus demand on claims account. We begin with firms.

II. Firms

1. The Firm Balance Sheet

The asset of firms is physical capital stock S valued at its current price P. The liability of firms is stockholders' equity Q_s valued at the current market price of shares Π_s. In nominal terms, then, firm wealth is

$$V_f \equiv PS - \Pi_s Q_s \tag{9.3}$$

2. The Firm Budget Constraint

The only part of current production in need of financing is the part not sold to households and government—that is, investment. So the deficit to be financed is physical investment I times its price P.

For any sector the budget constraint says that a deficit on goods account must equal supply minus demand on claims account. Firms supply claims on themselves in the form of dividend-bearing shares but demand no claims. In nominal terms, the firm budget constraint is

$$IP = \Pi_s \frac{dQ_s}{dt} \equiv \Pi_s g_{Qs} Q_s \tag{9.4}$$

3. Rate of Change in Firm Real Wealth

Divide firm nominal wealth 9.3 by P, write firm real wealth V_f/P, and differentiate with respect to time:

$$\frac{d(V_f/P)}{dt} \equiv \frac{dS}{dt} - \frac{d(\Pi_s Q_s/P)}{dt}$$

$$\equiv I - (g_{\Pi s} + g_{Qs} - g_P)\Pi_s Q_s/P \tag{9.5}$$

Multiply the nominal firm budget constraint 9.4 by $-1/P$, insert the result into the rate of change of firm real wealth 9.5, and write the latter as

$$\frac{d(V_f/P)}{dt} = (g_P - g_{\Pi s})\Pi_s Q_s/P \tag{9.6}$$

or, in English, the rate of change in firm real wealth equals real stockholders' equity times the difference between the rate of inflation and the rate of appreciation of shares.

Let firms engage in four activities: production, hiring, pricing, and investment.

4. Production, Hiring, and Pricing

Let firms apply the Cobb-Douglas production function

$$X = aL^{\alpha}S^{\beta} \tag{9.7}$$

where $0 < \alpha < 1$; $0 < \beta < 1$; $\alpha + \beta = 1$; and $a > 0$ and growing with time, representing technological progress. Let profit maximization under pure competition equalize real wage rate and physical marginal productivity of labor:

$$\frac{w}{P} = \frac{\partial X}{\partial L} = \alpha \frac{X}{L} \tag{9.8}$$

Two things follow. First, multiply 9.8 by PL and write the wage bill

$$W \equiv wL = \alpha PX \tag{9.9}$$

Second, rearrange 9.8 and express neoclassical mark-up pricing as

$$P = \frac{wL}{\alpha X} \tag{9.8}$$

or, in English, neoclassical price P equals per-unit labor cost wL/X marked up in the proportion $1/\alpha$. Differentiate 9.8 with respect to time and find our price equation

$$g_P = g_w + g_L - g_X \tag{9.10}$$

Once priced, physical output becomes national income. Let capital stock be immortal, so we may ignore capital consumption allowances and define national income as the money value of physical output

$$Y \equiv PX \tag{9.11}$$

We already found labor's share of it. To find capital's share, define physical marginal productivity of capital stock as

$$\kappa \equiv \frac{\partial X}{\partial S} = \beta \frac{X}{S} \qquad (9.12)$$

multiply by PS, and write the profits bill before tax

$$Z = \kappa PS = \beta PX \qquad (9.13)$$

Let profits be taxed only once—that is, when earned. Firms supplied no claims other than dividend-bearing shares. Ignore undistributed earnings. Then all aftertax profits are paid out as dividends.

$$(1 - T)\kappa PS = \delta Q_s \qquad (9.14)$$

The physical unit of shares is arbitrary. Let one physical unit of shares always be issued to finance one physical unit of capital stock, then

$$S = Q_s \qquad (9.15)$$

hence

$$(1 - T)\kappa P = \delta \qquad (9.16)$$

5. Investment

Let N be the present net worth of new capital stock S installed by an entrepreneur. Let his desired capital stock be the size of stock maximizing present net worth. A first-order condition for a maximum is

$$n \equiv \frac{\partial N}{\partial S} = 0 \qquad (9.17)$$

To find desired capital stock, proceed as follows. Let entrepreneurs be purely competitive, then price P of output is beyond their control. At time t, then, aftertax marginal value productivity of capital stock is $(1 - T)\kappa(t)P(t)$.

Let there be a market in which money may be placed or borrowed at the stationary nominal rate of interest r. Let interest earnings be taxed and interest expense be tax-deductible. Then money may be placed or borrowed at the aftertax rate $(1 - T)r$. Let that rate be applied when discounting future cash flows. As seen from the present time τ, then, aftertax marginal value productivity of capital stock is $(1 - T)\kappa(t)P(t)e^{-(1 - T)r(t - \tau)}$. Define present gross worth of another physical unit of capital stock as the present worth of all future aftertax marginal value productivities over its entire useful life:

$$k(\tau) \equiv \int_\tau^\infty (1 - T)\kappa(t)P(t)e^{-(1 - T)r(t - \tau)}dt \tag{9.18}$$

Let entrepreneurs expect physical marginal productivity of capital stock to be growing at the stationary rate g_κ:

$$\kappa(t) = \kappa(\tau)e^{g_\kappa(t - \tau)} \tag{9.19}$$

and price of output to be growing at the stationary rate g_P:

$$P(t) = P(\tau)e^{g_P(t - \tau)} \tag{9.20}$$

Insert these into 9.18, define

$$\rho \equiv (1 - T)r - (g_\kappa + g_P) \tag{9.21}$$

and write the integral 9.18 as

$$k(\tau) = \int_\tau^\infty (1 - T)\kappa(\tau)P(\tau)e^{-\rho(t - \tau)}dt$$

Neither $(1 - T)$, $\kappa(\tau)$, nor $P(\tau)$ is a function of t; hence, they may be taken outside the integral sign. Our g_κ, g_P, and r were all said to be stationary; hence the coefficient ρ of t is stationary, too. Assume $\rho > 0$. As a result find the integral to be

$$k = (1 - T)\kappa P/\rho \tag{9.22}$$

Find present net worth of another physical unit of capital stock as its gross worth minus its price:

$$n \equiv k - P = [(1 - T)\kappa/\rho - 1]P \tag{9.23}$$

Apply our first-order condition 9.17 to our result 9.23. Desired capital stock is the size of stock for which the present net worth of another physical unit of capital stock equals zero, or

$$(1 - T)\kappa = \rho \tag{9.24}$$

At first sight—incredibly!—it seems that taxation stimulates investment. Insert the definition 9.21 into the result 9.24, divide by $1 - T$, and write it as

$$\kappa = r - (g_\kappa + g_P)/(1 - T) \qquad (9.21, 9.24)$$

Since $0 < T < 1$ and since therefore $(g_\kappa + g_P)/(1 - T) > g_\kappa + g_P$, then if nothing else were different the desired physical marginal productivity κ of capital stock would be lower with taxation than without. That, in turn, could be accomplished only by a desired capital stock and investment larger with taxation than without. Taxation stimulates investment! Something else, however, will be different—that is, the rates of interest, as we shall see in section 9.VII.4.

Finally take equations 9.12 and 9.24 together and find desired capital stock

$$S = (1 - T)\beta X/\rho \qquad (9.25)$$

In accordance with the definition 9.2, differentiate desired capital stock 9.25 with respect to time, and write desired investment

$$I \equiv \frac{dS}{dt} = (1 - T)\beta g_X X/\rho \qquad (9.26)$$

If we think of 9.25 and 9.26 as being derived for an individual entrepreneur, then everything except X on their right-hand sides is common to all entrepreneurs. Factor out all common factors, sum over all entrepreneurs, then X becomes national physical output, and 9.25 and 9.26 become national desired capital stock and investment, respectively. Both are in inverse proportion to ρ. What is ρ? In equation 9.42, we shall see that as defined by 9.21 ρ is the dividend yield—the cost of equity financing. In solutions 9.74 and 9.85, we shall see that $g_\kappa = 0$; consequently ρ is also the aftertax real rate of interest—the cost of debt financing.

III. Households

1. The Household Balance Sheet

The assets of households are the desired holdings D_m, D_b, and D_s of money, bonds, and shares, respectively, valued at their current prices. By definition the price of money is unity. The prices of bonds and shares are Π_b and Π_s, respectively. The liabilities of households are none. In nominal terms, then, household wealth is

$$V_h \equiv D_m + \Pi_b D_b + \Pi_s D_s \qquad (9.27)$$

2. The Household Budget Constraint

Ignore undistributed earnings. Then all national income becomes personal income, and disposable income will equal national income minus government gross receipts plus government transfer payments to persons, subsidies, and interest paid by government. Or, ignoring what the government collects with one hand only to pay back with the other, disposable income simply equals national income minus government net receipts. But in this chapter, the bond supply Q_b is an important parameter, and interest paid by government iQ_b must appear explicitly. Define tax revenue R as government net receipts before interest paid by government and write money disposable income before capital gains

$$y \equiv Y + iQ_b - R \tag{9.28}$$

Saving is the negative of a deficit defined as consumption expenditure CP minus money disposable income before capital gains y. For any sector, the budget constraint says that a deficit on goods account must equal supply minus demand on claims account. Households supply no claims on themselves but demand noninterest-bearing money, interest-bearing bonds, and dividend-bearing shares. In nominal terms the household budget constraint is

$$CP - y = -\frac{dD_m}{dt} - \Pi_b \frac{dD_b}{dt} - \Pi_s \frac{dD_s}{dt}$$

$$\equiv -g_{Dm}D_m - \Pi_b g_{Db}D_b - \Pi_s g_{Ds}D_s \tag{9.29}$$

3. Rate of Change in Household Real Wealth

Divide household nominal wealth 9.27 by P, write household real wealth V_h/P, and differentiate with respect to time:

$$\frac{d(V_h/P)}{dt} \equiv \frac{d(D_m/P)}{dt} + \frac{d(\Pi_b D_b/P)}{dt} + \frac{d(\Pi_s D_s/P)}{dt}$$

$$\equiv (g_{Dm} - g_P)D_m/P + (g_{\Pi b} + g_{Db} - g_P)\Pi_b D_b/P$$

$$+ (g_{\Pi s} + g_{Ds} - g_P)\Pi_s D_s/P_P \tag{9.30}$$

Multiply the nominal household budget constraint 9.29 by $-1/P$, insert the result into the rate of change of household real wealth 9.30, and write the latter as

$$\frac{d(V_h/P)}{dt} = [y - g_P D_m + (g_{\Pi b} - g_P)\Pi_b D_b$$

$$+ (g_{\Pi s} - g_P)\Pi_s D_s]/P - C \tag{9.31}$$

or, in English, the rate of change of household real wealth equals real savings out of real disposable income after capital gains.

Let households engage in four activities: portfolio holding, consumption, work, and pricing the work.

4. Portfolio Holding: The Price of Bonds

At time t let an immortal bond be paying the interest $i(t)$ dollars per annum. Because interest earnings are taxed, the aftertax interest payment is $(1 - T)i(t)$. Because money may be placed or borrowed at the aftertax rate $(1 - T)r$, that rate should be applied when discounting future cash flows. As seen from the present time τ, then, the aftertax interest payment is worth $(1 - T)i(t)e^{-(1 - T)r(t - \tau)}$. Define the present gross worth of the bond as the present worth of all its future aftertax interest payments over its entire life:

$$k_b(\tau) \equiv \int_\tau^\infty (1 - T)i(t)e^{-(1-T)r(t - \tau)}dt \tag{9.32}$$

The interest payment is stationary:

$$i(t) = i(\tau) \tag{9.33}$$

Insert 9.33 into 9.32 and write the latter as

$$k_b(\tau) \equiv \int_\tau^\infty (1 - T)i(\tau)e^{-(1-T)r(t - \tau)}dt$$

Neither $(1 - T)$ nor $i(\tau)$ is a function of t; hence, they may be taken outside the integral sign. Our r was said to be stationary; hence the coefficient r of t is stationary. Assume $r > 0$ and find the integral to be

$$k_b = i/r \tag{9.34}$$

Find present net worth of the bond as its gross worth minus its price:

$$n_b \equiv k_b - \Pi_b = i/r - \Pi_b$$

Because equation 9.33 is virtually certain, the net worth will be common to virtually all bondholders. If $\Pi_b > i/r$ net worth will be negative, virtually all bondholders would wish to sell, and excess supply would lower price. If

$$\Pi_b = i/r \qquad (9.35)$$

net worth will be zero, and bondholders would be induced neither to buy nor to sell. If $\Pi_b < i/r$ net worth will be positive, bondholders would wish to buy, and excess demand would raise price. The price 9.35 alone is compatible with zero excess demand for bonds; hence, it is the equilibrium price.

The price of a bond, then, is a capitalization of its current before-tax interest payment i, and the capitalization factor is $1/r$ or the reciprocal of the before-tax nominal rate of interest. At first sight, the tax rate T seems to have disappeared from 9.35. Can the price of bonds really be invariant with taxation? Of course not! As we shall see in section 9.VII.4, an economy with a higher tax rate T will also have a higher before-tax nominal rate of interest r and hence a lower price of bonds.

5. Portfolio Holding: The Price of Shares

At time t let an immortal share be paying the dividend $\delta(t)$ dollars per annum. Because profits are taxed only once—that is, when earned—the dividend payment $\delta(t)$ is an aftertax payment. Because money may be placed or borrowed at the aftertax rate $(1 - T)r$, that rate should be applied when discounting future cash flows. As seen from the present time τ, then, the aftertax dividend payment is worth $\delta(t)e^{-(1-T)r(t-\tau)}$. Define present gross worth of the share as the present worth of all its future aftertax dividend payments over its entire life:

$$k_s(\tau) \equiv \int_\tau^\infty \delta(t)e^{-(1-T)r(t - \tau)}dt \qquad (9.36)$$

Let the shareholder expect the dividend payment to be growing at the stationary rate g_δ:

$$\delta(t) = \delta(\tau)e^{g_\delta(t-\tau)} \qquad (9.37)$$

Insert 9.37 into 9.36 and write the latter as

$$k_s(\tau) \equiv \int_\tau^\infty \delta(\tau)e^{-[(1-T)r - g_\delta](t - \tau)}dt$$

Here $\delta(\tau)$ is not a function of t; hence it may be taken outside the integral sign. Our g_δ and r were said to be stationary; hence the coefficient $[(1 - T)r - g_\delta]$ of t is stationary. Assume $(1 - T)r - g_\delta > 0$ and find the integral to be

$$k_s = \delta/[(1 - T)r - g_\delta)] \qquad (9.38)$$

Find present net worth of the share as its gross worth minus its price:

$$n_s \equiv k_s - \Pi_s = \delta/[(1 - T)r - g_\delta] - \Pi_s$$

Let most shareholders have the expectation 9.37; then the net worth will be common to most shareholders. If $\Pi_s > \delta/[(1 - T)r - g_\delta]$ net worth will be negative, shareholders would wish to sell, and excess supply would never lower price. If

$$\Pi_s = \delta/[(1 - T)r - g_\delta] \qquad (9.39)$$

net worth will be zero, and shareholders would be induced neither to buy nor to sell. If $\Pi_s < \delta/[(1 - T)r - g_\delta]$ net worth will be positive, shareholders would wish to buy, and excess demand would raise price. The price 9.39 alone is compatible with zero excess demand for shares; hence it is the equilibrium price.

Take a closer look at the denominator $(1 - T)r - g_\delta$ of 9.39. Recall that one physical unit of shares was always issued to finance one physical unit of capital stock. With 9.15 inserted into it, 9.14 collapsed into

$$(1 - T)\kappa P = \delta \qquad (9.40)$$

Differentiate 9.40 with respect to time, recall that T is stationary, and find

$$g_\delta = g_\kappa + g_P \qquad (9.41)$$

Insert 9.41 into the denominator of 9.39, use the definition 9.21, and write the equilibrium price of shares

$$\Pi_s = \delta/\rho \qquad (9.42)$$

So the price of a share is a capitalization of its current dividend payment δ, and the capitalization factor is $1/\rho$. Rearrange and realize that, as defined by 9.21, ρ is the dividend yield—the cost of equity capital:

$$\rho = \delta/\Pi_s \qquad (9.42)$$

6. Portfolio Holding: Rates of Aftertax Real Return

Expressed as dollars per physical unit of asset per unit of time, the aftertax nominal return on an asset is the sum of its aftertax earnings and its appreciation—that is, for money, bonds, and shares:

$$0 + 0 \qquad (9.43)$$

$$(1 - T)i + \frac{d\Pi_b}{dt} \qquad (9.44)$$

$$\delta + \frac{d\Pi_s}{dt} \qquad (9.45)$$

Divide by the prices 1, Π_b, and Π_s of the three assets, respectively; use 9.1; and express the rates of aftertax nominal return as the pure numbers per unit of time $0 + 0$, $(1 - T)i/\Pi_b + g_{\Pi b}$, and $\delta/\Pi_s + g_{\Pi s}$, respectively. Finally, subtract the rate of inflation g_P to find the rates of aftertax real return. But, first, the interest amount i and the nominal interest rate r were assumed to be stationary. Consequently, differentiation of 9.35 with respect to time shows that

$$g_{\Pi b} = 0 \qquad (9.46)$$

Second, insert 9.24 into 9.16 and find $P = \delta/\rho$. Compare with 9.42 and find $P = \Pi_s$. Differentiate with respect to time and find

$$g_P = g_{\Pi s} \qquad (9.47)$$

Insert 9.35, 9.42, 9.46, and 9.47 and write the three rates of aftertax real return:

$$0 + 0 - g_P = -g_P \qquad (9.48)$$

$$(1 - T)i/\Pi_b + g_{\Pi b} - g_P = (1 - T)r - g_P = \rho \qquad (9.49)$$

$$\delta/\Pi_s + g_{\Pi s} - g_P = \rho, \qquad (9.50)$$

respectively. In other words, when priced at 9.35 and 9.42, bonds and shares yield the same rates of aftertax real return ρ and are in that sense perfect substitutes.[1]

7. Portfolio Holding: The Demand for Money

Let the demand for money be a function of money national income *plus* government interest bill and of the aftertax nominal rate of interest:

$$D_m = m(Y + iQ_b)[(1 - T)r]^\mu \tag{9.51}$$

where $\mu < 0$ and $m > 0$.

The demand for an asset should be lower the higher the rates of aftertax real return on alternative assets. The demand for an asset should be higher the higher the rate of aftertax real return on the asset itself. In the case of money is it? Because $\mu < 0$, the demand for money is lower the higher the aftertax *nominal* rate of interest $(1 - T)r$. But the aftertax nominal rate of interest $(1 - T)r$ is the sum of the rate of aftertax real return ρ and the rate of inflation g_P: $(1 - T)r = \rho + g_P$. As we just saw in 9.49 and 9.50, the former term ρ is the rate of aftertax real return on the two alternative assets, bonds and shares. Because $\mu < 0$, the demand for money is indeed lower the higher the rates of aftertax real return on alternative assets! Because $\mu < 0$, the demand for money is also lower the higher the rate of inflation g_P. Consequently, the demand for money is *higher* the higher the *negative*, $-g_P$, of the rate of inflation. As we just saw in 9.48, that negative is the rate of aftertax real return on money itself. So the demand for money is indeed higher the higher the rate of aftertax real return on money itself!

8. Consumption

The second activity of households was consumption, and we build a consumption function separating income from nonwealth and income from wealth. Insert the tax-revenue function 9.63 into the definition 9.28 of money disposable income before capital gains and write it

$$y = (1 - T)(Y + iQ_b) \tag{9.52}$$

Assuming $\alpha + \beta = 1$, section 9.II.4 found the wage and profits shares 9.9 and 9.13 of national income 9.11 summing to the latter, as they should:

$$W + Z = Y \tag{9.53}$$

Insert 9.53 into 9.52 and write money disposable income before capital gains as

$$y = (1 - T) (W + Z + iQ_b) \tag{9.54}$$

The square bracket of 9.31 above was money disposable income after capital gains. After insertion of 9.46 and 9.47 it will collapse into

$$[y - g_P(D_m + \Pi_b D_b)]$$

Into that insert our result 9.54 and write real disposable income after (negative) capital gains as

$$[(1 - T) (W + Z + iQ_b) - g_P(D_m + \Pi_b D_b)]/P \tag{9.55}$$

Here $(1 - T)W/P$ is real disposable income from nonwealth, and all the rest is real disposable income from wealth. Multiply each of the two terms by its own propensity to consume and write our consumption function

$$C = c_1(1 - T)W/P$$

$$+ c_2[(1 - T) (Z + iQ_b) - g_P(D_m + \Pi_b D_b)]/P \tag{9.56}$$

where $0 < c_i < 1$. Consumption is a weighted sum of income from nonwealth and wealth. If the weights c_1 and c_2 differ, the presence of wealth will make the average overall propensity to consume differ from what it would have been in the absence of wealth. Our function 9.56, then, is the natural way to include wealth as an argument in the consumption function.

9. Working and Pricing the Work

The third household activity is work, and let labor employed be the proportion λ of available labor force:

$$L = \lambda F \tag{9.57}$$

where $0 < \lambda < 1$, and λ is so far not a function of time.

The fourth household activity is pricing the work. Within their province but tempered by unemployment, labor unions according to Phillips (1958) will seek a relative gain by raising the money wage rate. We write a modern Phillips function by subtracting employment 9.57 from available labor force F, finding the unemployment fraction to be $1 - \lambda$, and incorporating labor's inflationary expectations g_P:

$$g_w = p(1 - \lambda)^\pi + \phi g_P \tag{9.58}$$

where $\phi > 0$; $\pi < 0$; and $p > 0$ and so far not a function of time. Here the vertical axis is an asymptote: for $1 - \lambda \to 0$, $\lim g_w = \infty$. A horizontal line above the horizontal axis is another asymptote: for $1 - \lambda \to \infty$, $\lim g_w = \phi g_P$. The function 9.58 looks like a rectangular hyperbola and is one if $\pi = -1$. Its curvature describes the sensitivity of inflation to the unemployment fraction $1 - \lambda$. The employment fraction λ is Eckstein's "state of demand" (1981). The inflationary potential p is Eckstein's "shock" and may reflect shocks such as the food and oil shocks of the seventies but may also reflect institutional arrangements such as minimum wage rates or the rate and the maximum period of unemployment compensation.

IV. Government

1. The Government Balance Sheet

Government-owned physical stock, such as highways and universities, is not priced in any market and hence is ignored. The liabilities of government are noninterest-bearing money M, by definition priced at unity, and interest-bearing bonds Q_b priced at Π_b. In nominal terms, then, government wealth is

$$V_g \equiv -M - \Pi_b Q_b \qquad (9.59)$$

2. The Government Budget Constraint

The fiscal deficit is the money value of government purchase of goods and services plus the payment of interest on government bonds minus tax revenue, or $GP + iQ_b - R$.

For any sector the budget constraint says that a deficit on goods account must equal supply minus demand on claims account. Government supplies claims on itself in the form of noninterest-bearing money and interest-bearing bonds but demands no claims. In nominal terms, the government budget constraint is

$$GP + iQ_b - R = \frac{dM}{dt} + \Pi_b \frac{dQ_b}{dt} \equiv g_M M + \Pi_b g_{Qb} Q_b \qquad (9.60)$$

3. Rate of Change in Government Real Wealth

Divide government nominal wealth 9.59 by P, write government real wealth V_g/P, and differentiate with respect to time:

$$\frac{d(V_g/P)}{dt} \equiv \frac{-d(M/P)}{dt} - \frac{d(\Pi_b Q_b/P)}{dt}$$

$$\equiv -(g_M - g_P)M/P - (g_{\Pi b} + g_{Qb} - g_P)\Pi_b Q_b/P \qquad (9.61)$$

Multiply the nominal government budget constraint 9.60 by $-1/P$, insert the result into the rate of change of government real wealth from 9.61, and write the latter as

$$\frac{d(V_g/P)}{dt} = -(G + iQ_b/P - R/P)$$

$$+ g_P M/P + (g_P - g_{\Pi b})\Pi_b Q_b/P \qquad (9.62)$$

or, in English, the rate of change in government real wealth equals minus real fiscal deficit plus inflationary erosion $g_P M/P$ of government real non-interest-bearing debt plus inflationary erosion $g_P \Pi_b Q_b/P$ of government real interest-bearing debt minus appreciation $g_{\Pi b}\Pi_b Q_b/P$, if any, of bonds. In even plainer English, the deterioration of government real wealth caused by a real fiscal deficit is tempered by the inflationary erosion of government real debt.

4. Government Activities

Let government engage in three activities: purchasing goods and services, servicing the government debt, and collecting taxes. The money value of government purchase of goods and services is GP. Let government bonds be perpetuities, each paying the stationary amount of interest i dollars per annum. Q_b is the physical quantity of outstanding government bonds. The government interest bill will then be the amount of interest per annum per bond times that quantity, or iQ_b. Let tax revenue R be government net receipts before interest paid by government. Let tax revenue be in proportion to money national income plus government interest bill:

$$R = T(Y + iQ_b) \qquad (9.63)$$

where $0 < T < 1$.

V. Equilibrium

1. Summing the Nominal Budget Constraints

Insert the definitions 9.11 and 9.28 of money national and money disposable income into the household budget constraint 9.29 and sum the three nominal budget constraints 9.4, 9.29, and 9.60:

$$(C + I + G - X)P =$$

$$-\left(\frac{dD_m}{dt} - \frac{dM}{dt}\right) - \Pi_b\left(\frac{dD_b}{dt} - \frac{dQ_b}{dt}\right) - \Pi_s\left(\frac{dD_s}{dt} - \frac{dQ_s}{dt}\right) \quad (9.64)$$

or, in English, excess demand in the goods market equals minus excess demand in the money market minus excess demand in the bond market minus excess demand in the share market.

2. Equilibria

Goods-market equilibrium requires the supply of goods to equal the demand for them:

$$X = C + I + G \qquad (9.65)$$

Money-market equilibrium requires the supply of money to equal the demand for it:

$$M = D_m \qquad (9.66)$$

Sections 9.III.4–9.III.6 showed that when priced at 9.35 and 9.42, bonds and shares would yield the same rate of aftertax real return ρ and be perfect substitutes. In that case, the bond and share markets could be consolidated into one single security market and Walras' Law applied to 9.64: Goods-market equilibrium and money-market equilibrium imply security-market equilibrium.

VI. Steady-State Equilibrium Growth Solutions

1. Steady-State Growth

By differentiating equations 9.1 through 9.66 with respect to time, the reader may convince himself that they are satisfied by the following steady-state growth solutions:

$$g_C = g_X \tag{9.67}$$

$$g_{Db} = g_{Qb} \tag{9.68}$$

$$g_{Dm} = g_M \tag{9.69}$$

$$g_{Ds} = g_{Qs} \tag{9.70}$$

$$g_\delta = g_P \tag{9.71}$$

$$g_G = g_X \tag{9.72}$$

$$g_I = g_X \tag{9.73}$$

$$g_\kappa = g_X - g_S \tag{9.74}$$

$$g_L = g_F \tag{9.75}$$

$$g_M = g_Y \tag{9.76}$$

$$g_P = \frac{p(1-\lambda)^\pi - g_a/\alpha}{1-\phi} \tag{9.77}$$

$$g_{\Pi b} = 0 \tag{9.78}$$

$$g_{\Pi s} = g_P \tag{9.79}$$

$$g_{Qb} = g_Y \tag{9.80}$$

$$g_{Qs} = g_X \tag{9.81}$$

$$g_R = g_Y \tag{9.82}$$

$$g_r = 0 \tag{9.83}$$

$$g_\rho = 0 \tag{9.84}$$

$$g_s = g_X \tag{9.85}$$

$$g_w = g_Y \tag{9.86}$$

$$g_w = \frac{p(1 - \lambda)^\pi - \phi g_a/\alpha}{1 - \phi}$$
(9.87)

$$g_X = g_a/\alpha + g_F$$
(9.88)

$$g_Y = g_P + g_X$$
(9.89)

$$g_y = g_Y$$
(9.90)

$$g_z = g_Y$$
(9.91)

Our growth was steady-state growth, for no right-hand side of our solutions 9.67 through 9.91 was a function of time. The employment fraction λ and the inflationary potential p were assumed not to be. In principle, then, our solutions 9.67 through 9.91 define infinitely many steady-state equilibrium growth tracks, each with its own employment fraction λ and inflationary potential p.

2. System Has Self-Fulfilling Expectations: Eckstein's Core

Our system implies self-fulfilling expectations; we used the same symbol for the expected and realized values of any variable, implying equality between the two. Is such equality always possible? Yes, if the system has a set of solutions. It has the set 9.67 through 9.91.

Consequently our price-wage equilibrium implies, first, that if entrepreneurs expect labor to adopt the solution value 9.87 of the rate of growth of the money wage rate, then the entrepreneurs will adopt the solution value 9.77 of the rate of growth of price. Second, if labor expects entrepreneurs to do so, labor will adopt the solution value 9.87 of the rate of growth of the money wage rate.

Eckstein (1981) neatly separates three sources of inflation: core, demand, and shock. Let us use his distinction to characterize our steady-state equilibrium growth tracks defined by 9.67 through 9.91. Each track has its own employment fraction λ, which is Eckstein's state of demand. Each track has its own inflationary potential p, which is Eckstein's shock. All tracks have a common core defined by Eckstein (1981:8) as "the rate that would occur on the economy's long-term growth path, provided the path were free of shocks, and the state of demand were neutral in the sense that markets were in long-run equilibrium."

3. Nominal and Real Variables

Of solutions in which the employment fraction λ and the inflationary potential p are present, there will be infinitely many. We find g_P and g_w, and with them λ and p, to be present in the growth-rate solutions for the thirteen nominal variables D_b, D_m, δ, M, P, Π_s, Q_b, R, W, w, Y, y, and Z.

But some of our growth-rate solutions *are* unique. We find g_P and g_w, and with them λ and p, to be absent from the growth-rate solutions for the twelve real variables C, D_s, G, I, κ, L, Π_b, Q_s, r, ρ, S, and X. We shall now find them absent from the growth-rate solution for the real wage rate.

4. "Natural" Rate of Unemployment Not Unique

Subtract 9.77 from 9.87 to find the growth-rate solution for the real wage rate

$$g_{w/P} \equiv g_w - g_P = g_a/\alpha \tag{9.92}$$

Friedman (1968:8) defined a "natural" rate of unemployment as one at which "real wage rates are tending on the average to rise at a 'normal' secular rate, that is, at a rate that can be indefinitely maintained so long as capital formation, technological improvement, etc., remain on their long-run trends." But our real wage rate was growing like that for any value of the employment fraction λ: λ disappeared from 9.92! Friedman's natural rate is not unique.

5. System Not Normally "Accelerationist"

Write our price and wage equations 9.92 and 9.58 with g_w explicit:

$$g_w = g_a/\alpha + g_P \tag{9.92}$$

$$g_w = p(1-\lambda)^\pi + \phi g_P \tag{9.58}$$

and plot them in figure 9–1, having g_w on the vertical axis and g_P on the horizontal axis. The price equation 9.92 will then appear as a single straight line with the intercept g_a/α and the slope one. The wage equations 9.58 will appear as a family of straight lines with the intercepts $p(1-\lambda)^\pi$

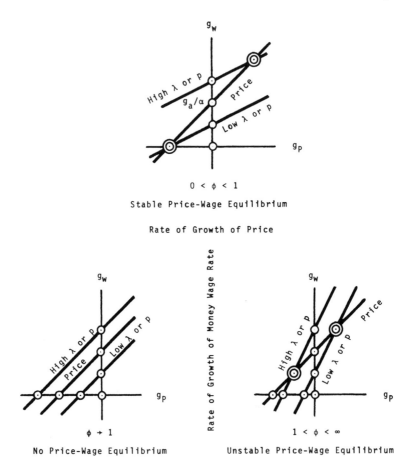

Figure 9–1. The Price-Wage Equilibrium. Three Possibilities

and the slope ϕ. Our price-wage equilibrium 9.77 and 9.87 is represented graphically by the intersection between the price-equation line and a wage-equation line. Intersection points are marked by double circles in figure 9–1. Consider the following three possibilities.

First, let $0 < \phi < 1$. Here the wage equation appears as a family of positively sloped lines with the intercepts $p(1 - \lambda)^\pi$. Their slope ϕ is less than one; hence they intersect the price-equation line from above, and the equilibria are stable. If, say, labor overshoots because it expects a g_P higher than the equilibrium value 9.77, entrepreneurs will respond along their price-equation line and raise price less than labor expected. Labor will go from there and respond along its wage-equation line and overshoot less.

And so it goes. The parties are moving back toward the equilibrium point. Again, if $p(1 - \lambda)^\pi$ is less than, equal to, or greater than g_a/α, the rate of inflation g_P will be negative, zero, or positive, respectively. The rate of inflation is higher the higher the employment fraction λ and the inflationary potential p.

Second, let $\phi \rightarrow 1$. Now the wage equation approaches a family of lines with unitary slope and the intercepts $p(1 - \lambda)^\pi$. All have the same slope as the price-equation line. If $p(1 - \lambda)^\pi$ is less than, equal to, or greater than g_a/α, there will be hyperdeflation with no equilibrium, infinitely many equilibria, or hyperinflation with no equilibrium, respectively. The limits of equation 9.77 and 9.87 are

$$\lim_{\phi \to 1} g_P = \lim_{\phi \to 1} g_w = \pm\infty$$

Third, let $1 < \phi < \infty$. The wage equation appears as a family of positively sloped lines with the intercepts $p(1 - \lambda)^\pi$. But now their slope is greater than one; hence they intersect the price-equation line from below, and the equilibria are unstable. If, say, labor overshoots because it expects a g_P higher than the equilibrium value 9.77, entrepreneurs will respond along their price-equation line and raise price more than labor expected. Labor will go from there and respond along its wage-equation line and overshoot even more. And so it goes. The parties are now veering farther and farther away from the equilibrium point. Again, the rate of inflation will depend on the employment fraction λ and the coefficient p but in an upside-down way. Now, if $p(1 - \lambda)^\pi$ is less than, equal to, or greater than g_a/α, the rate of inflation g_P will be positive, zero, or negative, respectively. In other words, the rate of inflation is *lower* the higher the employment fraction λ and the inflationary potential p!

We conclude that our system will be "accelerationist," generate hyperinflation or hyperdeflation, only in the second, limiting case $\phi \rightarrow 1$. That case is sometimes being defended by saying that in its absence, income distribution would be tampered with. But least of all believers in rational expectations can afford such a defense. All our double-circled price-wage equilibria in figure 9-1 are located on the single price-equation line. That means that with or without inflation labor can have—and will get—a real wage rate growing at the rate g_a/α, as equation 9.92 said. Income distribution is never tampered with!

6. Zero Inflation?

Zero inflation is at least thinkable—and we almost had it as late as twenty

years ago, in the 1961–1964 period. In our own model, for the solution
9.77 to be zero, its numerator would have to be zero. Consequently, the
fortuitous combination

$$p(1 - \lambda)^\pi = g_a/\alpha$$

of the employment fraction λ and the inflationary potential p would make
inflation zero. The set of solutions 9.67 through 9.91 defined infinitely many
steady-state equilibrium growth tracks. Each track had its own employment
fraction λ (Eckstein's demand) and its own inflationary potential p (Eckstein's shock). Consequently some of our steady-state equilibrium growth
tracks are zero-inflation tracks. Within our system, zero inflation is indeed
thinkable, if fortuitous!

More practically, we must now identify winners and losers in the inflation game.

7. Winners and Losers in the Inflation Game: Firms

Equation 9.6 found the rate of change in firm real wealth to equal real
stockholders' equity times the difference between the rate of inflation
and the rate of appreciation of shares. Into 9.6 insert our newly found
equilibrium solution 9.79 and write

$$\frac{d(V_f/P)}{dt} = 0 \qquad (9.93)$$

In steady-state equilibrium growth, then, firms are neither winners
nor losers. Their investment is matched by new equity of the same value, and
the appreciation of existing equity is matched by inflation.

8. Winners and Losers in the Inflation Game: Households

Equation 9.31 found the rate of change in household real wealth to equal
real savings out of real disposable income after capital gains. Into 9.31 insert
our newly found equilibrium solutions 9.78 and 9.79 and write it as

$$\frac{d(V_h/P)}{dt} = [y - g_P(D_m + \Pi_b D_b)]/P - C \qquad (9.94)$$

In steady-state equilibrium growth and inflation, then, households are losers in the sense that on capital account they suffer real capital losses on their money and bond holdings and make neither real capital gains nor losses on their share holdings. All expectations being self-fulfilling, however, all real capital gains and losses are fully foreseen, and portfolios adjusted accordingly. At high rates of inflation, in accordance with 9.51 money holdings are kept at a minimum, and in accordance with 9.35 bonds are acquired at bargain-basement prices.

Our steady-state equilibrium solution 9.79 said that the rates of growth of share and goods prices would be the same—and for that reason households made neither real capital gains nor losses on their share holdings. A historical illustration of an extreme case of 9.79 is given in figure 9–2. In the German hyperinflation from 1920 to 1923 share prices followed goods prices quite accurately into the trillions!

9. Winners and Losers in the Inflation Game: Government

Equation 9.62 found the rate of change in government real wealth to equal minus real fiscal deficit plus inflationary erosion $g_P M/P$ of government real noninterest-bearing debt plus inflationary erosion $g_P \Pi_b Q_b/P$ of government real interest-bearing debt minus appreciation $g_{\Pi b} \Pi_b Q_b/P$, if any, of bonds. Into 9.62 insert equilibrium solution 9.78 and write

$$\frac{d(V_g/P)}{dt} = -(G + iQ_b/P - R/P) + g_P(M/P + \Pi_b Q_b/P) \qquad (9.95)$$

In steady-state equilibrium growth and inflation, then, government is a winner in the sense that on capital account it makes real capital gains on its money and bond liabilities. Both are being eroded by inflation.

Again, a historical illustration of an extreme case may be useful. Figure 1–4 showed how the German World War One debt—and then some—was wiped out by the hyperinflation from 1920 to 1923.

10. Summing All Changes in Real Wealth

> *Geld ist bedrucktes Papier; dadurch, dass Papier seinen Wert verliert, gehen keine wirklichen Werte verloren. Sie wechseln nur die Hände.*[2]
> —Golo Mann (1961:28)

Zero excess demand in the money and securities markets requires desired holding to equal physical quantity outstanding for money, bonds, and

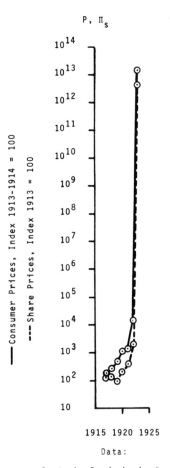

Figure 9–2. Consumer Prices and Share Prices in Hyperinflation, Germany, 1917–1923

shares—that is, $D_m = M$, $D_b = Q_b$, and $D_s = Q_s$. If we sum all changes in real wealth 9.93, 9.94, and 9.95, all capital gains and losses will cancel, and the rate of change in real wealth for the economy as a whole will collapse into

$$\frac{d(V/P)}{dt} \equiv \frac{d(V_f/P)}{dt} + \frac{d(V_h/P)}{dt} + \frac{d(V_g/P)}{dt}$$

$$= y/P - C - (G + iQ_b/P - R/P)$$

or, in English, the rate of change in economy-wide real wealth equals real household savings out of real disposable income before real capital gains minus real government deficit. In the sense that all capital gains and losses have cancelled, inflation is a zero-sum game—as observed by Golo Mann.

VII. Steady-State Equilibrium Level Solutions: Rates of Interest, Capital Coefficient, and Real Wage Rate

1. Government and Interest

Throughout this book, money and bond issues have been considered policy instruments. In equilibrium, households will be persuaded to hold whatever money and bonds the government has issued. What persuades them? The variable aftertax nominal rate of interest $(1 - T)r$ and with it the variable price Π_b of bonds will adjust to persuade households to hold whatever money and bonds the government has issued—no more, no less.

Playing on its instruments, then, the government may presumably affect interest rates. To see how, we must solve our system for their steady-state equilibrium levels.

2. The Aftertax Real Rate of Interest

In steady-state growth theory it is usually easier to find solutions for growth rates than for levels. Can we solve our system for the level of the aftertax real rate of interest ρ? Insert the goods-market equilibrium condition 9.65 into the left-hand side of the investment function 9.26 and write the aftertax real rate of interest as

$$\rho = \frac{(1 - T)\beta g_X X}{X - (C + G)}$$

Into the consumption function 9.56, insert the distributive shares 9.9 and 9.13, $D_m = M$, and $D_b = Q_b$ required by zero excess demand in the securities market. Now we have physical consumption C. To get physical government purchase G, insert the tax-revenue function 9.63 into the nominal government budget constraint 9.60 and divide by price P. Insert them into the denominator $X - (C + G)$. Finally, divide numerator and denominator alike by $(1 - T)X$, use 9.11 to write PX as Y, and write the aftertax real rate of interest

$$\rho = \beta g_X / A \qquad (9.96)$$

where

$$A \equiv 1 - (\alpha c_1 + \beta c_2)$$

$$- \frac{(g_M - c_2 g_P)M/Y + (g_{Qb} - c_2 g_P)\Pi_b Q_b/Y}{1 - T}$$

$$+ (1 - c_2)i Q_b/Y$$

Do we find government and its policy instruments present here? Let us inspect the three terms of A in turn.

The first term of A is $1 - (\alpha c_1 + \beta c_2)$. That would be the overall propensity to save real disposable income in an economy knowing neither government nor inflation. In such an economy there would be no negative capital gains due to inflation, and no saving would be absorbed by a government deficit. All saving would be available to finance investment, and the real rate of interest would simply be in direct proportion to the elasticity β of output with respect to capital stock and in inverse proportion to the propensity to save. As Fisher (1930:title page) said it so well in his subtitle, the real rate of interest would be "determined by impatience to spend income and opportunity to invest it." But our first term of A is not the only one.

The presence of the second term of A is the consequence of government deficits and inflation. First, had the budget been balanced, $g_M = g_{Qb} = 0$, the first terms of the coefficients of M/Y and $\Pi_b Q_b/Y$ would not have been there. Being there and being preceded by minus signs, they tell us that some saving otherwise available to finance investment is now being channeled into financing a government deficit. Second, had there been no inflation, $g_P = 0$, households would have suffered no negative capital gains from it, and the second terms $c_2 g_P$ of the coefficients of M/Y and $\Pi_b Q_b/Y$ would not have been there. Being there and being preceded by double minus signs, they tell us that the negative capital gains resulting from inflation are reducing consumption—that is, augmenting saving.

The presence of the third term of A is the consequence of accumulated government debt. Had there been no debt, $Q_b = 0$, and hence no interest income from it, the third term would not have been there. Being there and being preceded by a plus sign, it tells us that personal income exceeds national income by interest income from government debt, and that part of that excess is being saved. The government is giving as well as taking away.

Does A have a simple economic meaning, then? It has. Multiply both sides of 9.96 by $1 - T$, insert our investment function 9.26, find

$$(1 - T)A = I/X \qquad\qquad (9.26, 9.96)$$

and realize that $(1 - T)A$ is simply the fraction of output invested in an economy knowing government and inflation. Indeed government and its policy instruments are present in 9.96!

Equation 9.96 includes both the real and the nominal rate of interest. In its aftertax form, the real rate of interest appears visibly on the left-hand side. In its before-tax form the nominal rate of interest is hiding behind the price of bonds

$$\Pi_b = i/r \qquad (9.35)$$

In its aftertax form, the nominal rate of interest is hiding behind an important relationship between Q_b/Y and M/Y. Insert the money-market equilibrium condition 9.66 into the demand-for-money function 9.51, divide both sides by Y, rearrange, and write

$$(1 - T)r = [m(1 + iQ_b/Y)/(M/Y)]^{-1/\mu} \qquad (9.51, 9.66)$$

Let us call the proportion $(1 + iQ_b/Y)/(M/Y)$ a "bond-money ratio." A high bond-money ratio means that in its deficit financing, a government traditionally relies more on bonds than on money. A low bond-money ratio means that it traditionally relies more on money than on bonds. But whatever its tradition, in steady-state growth equilibrium the government will let its money and bond supplies grow in accordance with solutions 9.76 and 9.80—that is, at the same rates $g_M = g_{Qb} = g_Y$ as money national income. As a result, in such an equilibrium, the money-income ratio M/Y, the bond-income ratio Q_b/Y, the bond-money ratio $(1 + iQ_b/Y)/(M/Y)$, and with them the aftertax nominal rate of interest will all remain stationary. Whatever the government tradition is, a steady-state growth equilibrium will uphold it.

It follows equally clearly from 9.51 and 9.66 that unless the stationary level of the bond-money ratio $(1 + iQ_b/Y)/(M/Y)$ differs from one such steady-state growth equilibrium to another, the aftertax nominal rate of interest $(1 - T)r$ cannot differ. Because $\mu < 0$, a high bond-money ratio means a high aftertax nominal rate of interest, and a low bond-money ratio means a low aftertax nominal rate of interest.

Finally, the definition 9.21 relates the aftertax nominal rate of interest to the aftertax real rate:

$$(1 - T)r \equiv \rho + g_\kappa + g_P \qquad (9.21)$$

Allowing for all this we should like to know if and how, according to 9.96, ρ depends on inflation and taxation.

3. Sensitivity of Aftertax Real Rate of Interest to Inflation

Let us compare a more inflationary steady-state equilibrium growth track having a higher $g_M = g_{Qb} = g_Y$ to a less inflationary track. Will the aftertax real rate of interest ρ differ between the two tracks? To see if it will, we must differentiate 9.96 with respect to the rate of inflation g_P.

To make sure that all interest rates are free to vary, we must leave the bond-money ratio free to vary. We do that by inserting 9.21, 9.51, and 9.66 into 9.96 before the differentiation. But with those equations inserted into it, 9.96 will have the sum $\rho + g_\kappa + g_P$ raised to the power μ in it and will not permit an explicit solution for ρ. Implicit differentiation of 9.96, then, is our only way of establishing the sensitivity of ρ to g_P. There are two ways of leaving the bond-money ratio free to vary, and we try both.

The first way is to let M/Y adjust to Q_b/Y (lower M/Y; same Q_b/Y). Into A of 9.96 insert

$$M/Y = m(1 + iQ_b/Y)(\rho + g_\kappa + g_P)^\mu \qquad \text{(9.21), (9.51), (9.66)}$$

$$\Pi_b/(1 - T) = i/(\rho + g_\kappa + g_P) \qquad \text{(9.21), (9.35)}$$

$$g_M = g_{Qb} = g_Y = g_P + g_X \qquad \text{(9.76), (9.80), (9.89)}$$

but consider neither α, β, c_i, g_κ, g_X, i, m, μ, Q_b/Y, nor T a function of the rate of inflation g_P. Then differentiate 9.96 with respect to g_P. Upon the result, use 9.21, 9.35, 9.51, and 9.66 once again and write it as

$$\frac{\partial \rho}{\partial g_P} = -\beta g_X \frac{J_1 - (1 - c_2)(1 - T)(M/Y + \Pi_b Q_b/Y)}{A^2(1 - T)^2 + \beta g_X J_1} \qquad \text{(9.97a)}$$

where

$$J_1 \equiv [(1 - c_2)g_P + g_X](-\mu M/Y + \Pi_b Q_b/Y)/r$$

Using the following, not implausible, values[3]

$$A = 0.08$$
$$\alpha = 0.8$$
$$\beta = 0.2$$
$$c_1 = 0.95$$
$$c_2 = 0.75$$
$$g_\kappa = 0$$
$$g_P = 0.07$$
$$g_X = 0.02$$
$$iQ_b/Y = 0.024$$
$$M/Y = 0.17$$
$$\mu = -0.2$$

$$\Pi_b Q_b / Y = 0.15$$
$$r = 0.16$$
$$\rho = 0.05$$
$$T = 0.25$$

we find the sensitivity 9.97a of the aftertax real rate of interest to the rate of inflation to be 0.01789. So if the more inflationary growth track has a lower M/Y but the same Q_b/Y and has a one percentage point higher rate of inflation g_P, it will have a 0.01789 percentage point higher aftertax real rate of interest ρ. According to 9.21, it will then have a 1.01789 percentage point higher aftertax nominal rate of interest $(1 - T)r$ and a 1.3572 percentage point higher before-tax nominal rate of interest r.

The second way of leaving the bond-money ratio free to vary is to let Q_b/Y adjust to M/Y (higher Q_b/Y; same M/Y). Into A of 9.96 insert

$$Q_b/Y = \frac{M/Y}{im}(\rho + g_\kappa + g_P)^{-\mu} - \frac{1}{i} \qquad (9.21), (9.51), (9.66)$$

$$\Pi_b/(1 - T) = i/(\rho + g_\kappa + g_P) \qquad (9.21), (9.35)$$

$$g_M = g_{Qb} = g_Y = g_P + g_X \qquad (9.76), (9.80), (9.89)$$

but consider neither α, β, c_i, g_κ, g_X, i, M/Y, m, μ, nor T a function of the rate of inflation g_P. Then differentiate 9.96 with respect to g_P. Upon the result, use 9.21, 9.35, 9.51, and 9.66 once again and write it as

$$\frac{\partial \rho}{\partial g_P} = -\beta g_X \frac{J_2 - (1 - c_2)(1 - T)(M/Y + \Pi_b Q_b/Y)}{A^2(1 - T)^2 + \beta g_X J_2} \qquad (9.97b)$$

where

$$J_2 \equiv [(1 - c_2)g_P + g_X][\mu + (1 + \mu)iQ_b/Y]/r^2$$

$$-\mu(1 - c_2)(1 - T)(1 + iQ_b/Y)/r$$

For the previous list of numerical values, the sensitivity 9.97b of the aftertax real rate of interest to the rate of inflation is 0.09695. So if the more inflationary growth track has a higher Q_b/Y but the same M/Y and has a one percentage point higher rate of inflation g_P, it will have a 0.09695 percentage point higher aftertax real rate of interest ρ. According to 9.21, it will then have a 1.09695 percentage point higher aftertax nominal rate of interest $(1 - T)r$ and a 1.4626 percentage point higher before-tax nominal rate of interest r.

The sensitivities of the aftertax real rate of interest are small but magnify themselves into the sensitivities of both a nominal and a real variable. The nominal one is the before-tax nominal rate of interest, which is up by much more than the aftertax real rate is up and by a good bit more than the rate of inflation is up.

To see the other magnification, we must go back to our equilibrium condition 9.24 saying that the physical marginal productivity κ of capital stock must equal $\rho/(1 - T)$. Consequently, if the more inflationary growth track has, say, a 0.09695 percentage point higher aftertax real rate of interest ρ, it must have a 0.1292 percentage point higher physical marginal productivity κ of capital stock.

4. Sensitivity of Aftertax Real Rate of Interest to Taxation

Next, let us compare a high-tax equilibrium growth track to a low-tax track having the same $g_M = g_{Qb} = g_Y$. Will the aftertax real rate of interest ρ differ between the two tracks? To see if it will, we must differentiate 9.96 —again implicitly!—with respect to the tax rate T. Again, there are two ways of leaving the bond-money ratio free to vary, and we try both.

The first way is to let M/Y adjust to Q_b/Y (lower M/Y; same Q_b/Y). Into A of 9.96 insert

$$M/Y = m(1 + iQ_b/Y)(\rho + g_\kappa + g_P)^\mu \qquad (9.21),\ (9.51),\ (9.66)$$

$$\Pi_b/(1 - T) = i/(\rho + g_\kappa + g_P) \qquad (9.21),\ (9.35)$$

$$g_M = g_{Qb} = g_Y = g_P + g_X \qquad (9.76),\ (9.80),\ (9.89)$$

but consider neither α, β, c_i, g_κ, g_M, g_P, g_{Qb}, g_X, i, m, μ, nor Q_b/Y a function of the tax rate T. Then differentiate 9.96 with respect to T. Upon the result, use 9.21, 9.35, 9.51, and 9.66 once again and write it as

$$\frac{\partial \rho}{\partial T} = \beta g_X \frac{[(1 - c_2)g_P + g_X]M/Y}{A^2(1 - T)^2 + \beta g_X J_1} \qquad (9.98a)$$

where J_1 was defined in 9.97a. For the previous list of numerical values, the sensitivity 9.98a of the aftertax real rate of interest to the tax rate is 0.00676. So if the high-tax growth track has a lower M/Y but the same Q_b/Y and has a one percentage point higher tax rate T, it will have a 0.00676 percentage point higher aftertax real rate of interest ρ. According to 9.21, it will then have a 0.00676 percentage point higher aftertax nominal rate of interest $(1 - T)r$ and a 0.2254 percentage point higher before-tax nominal rate of interest r.

The second way of leaving the bond-money ratio free to vary is to let Q_b/Y adjust to M/Y (higher Q_b/Y; same M/Y). Into A of 9.96 insert

$$Q_b/Y = \frac{M/Y}{im} (\rho + g_\kappa + g_P)^{-\mu} - \frac{1}{i} \quad \text{(9.21), (9.51), (9.66)}$$

$$\Pi_b/(1 - T) = i/(\rho + g_\kappa + g_P) \quad \text{(9.21), (9.35)}$$

$$g_M = g_{Qb} = g_Y = g_P + g_X \quad \text{(9.76), (9.80), (9.89)}$$

but consider neither α, β, c_i, g_κ, g_M, g_P, g_{Qb}, g_X, i, M/Y, m, nor μ a function of the tax rate T. Then differentiate 9.96 with respect to T. Upon the result, use 9.21, 9.35, 9.51, and 9.66 once again and write it as

$$\frac{\partial \rho}{\partial T} = \beta g_X \frac{[(1 - c_2)g_P + g_X]M/Y}{A^2(1 - T)^2 + \beta g_X J_2} \quad \text{(9.98b)}$$

where J_2 was defined in 9.97b. For the previous list of numerical values, the sensitivity 9.98b of the aftertax real rate of interest to the tax rate is 0.00728. So if the high-tax growth track has a higher Q_b/Y but the same M/Y and has a one percentage point higher tax rate T, it will have a 0.00728 percentage point higher aftertax real rate of interest ρ. According to equation 9.21, it will then have a 0.00728 percentage point higher aftertax nominal rate of interest $(1 - T)r$ and a 0.2261 percentage point higher before-tax nominal rate of interest r.

The sensitivities of the aftertax real rate of interest are small but again magnify themselves into the sensitivities of both a nominal and a real variable. The nominal one is the before-tax nominal rate of interest, which is up by much more than the aftertax real rate is up (and the rate of inflation is not even up at all).

To see the second magnification, we again go back to our equilibrium condition 9.24, saying that the physical marginal productivity κ must equal $\rho/(1 - T)$. Now the higher the taxation, the higher the ρ and the smaller the fraction $1 - T$. Consequently, if the high-tax growth track has, say, a 0.00728 percentage point higher aftertax real rate of interest ρ, it must have a 0.09992 percentage point higher physical marginal productivity κ of capital stock. The latter is up by much more than the aftertax real rate of interest is up. As a result, the high-tax growth track must have a significantly lower desired capital stock and investment than the low-tax track. Our model does have a Feldstein Effect (1976)!

Having examined the level of the aftertax real rate of interest, let us examine two important ratios depending on it.

5. The Capital Coefficient

The capital coefficient is the ratio between the levels of physical capital stock and output. Rearrange 9.25 and write it

$$S/X = (1 - T)\beta/\rho \qquad (9.25)$$

which, according to 9.85 will be growing at the rate zero and in which ρ stands for 9.96 and is sensitive to inflation and taxation as just found. Higher inflation or taxation mean higher ρ, hence a lower capital coefficient. Higher taxation in addition means lower $1 - T$, hence an even lower capital coefficient. Something similar is true of another important ratio.

6. The Real Wage Rate

The real wage rate is the ratio between the levels of the money wage rate and price. Divide the production function 9.7 first by L, then by S and find

$$X/L = a(S/L)^\beta$$

$$X/S = a(L/S)^\alpha$$

Raise the latter equation to the power $1/\alpha$, rearrange, insert into the former equation, insert the result into 9.8, and write the level of the before-tax real wage rate

$$w/P = \alpha a^{1/\alpha}(S/X)^{\beta/\alpha}$$

Rearrange 9.25, insert it, and find the solution for the level of the before-tax real wage rate in an economy knowing government and inflation:

$$w/P = \alpha a^{1/\alpha}[(1 - T)\beta/\rho]^{\beta/\alpha} \qquad (9.99)$$

which will indeed be growing at the rate 9.92 and in which ρ stands for 9.96 and is sensitive to inflation and taxation as just found. Higher inflation or taxation mean higher ρ, hence lower before-tax real wage rate. Higher taxation in addition means lower $1 - T$, hence an even lower before-tax real wage rate. Notice that the T appearing in 9.99 came from 9.25 and is the tax on profits, not wages.

VIII. Nonsteady-State Growth: Crowding Out and Crowding In

1. Rate of Growth of Physical Capital Stock

Into the consumption function 9.56 insert the distributive shares 9.9 and 9.13, $D_m = M$, and $D_b = Q_b$ required by zero excess demand in the securities market. Now we have physical consumption C. To get physical government purchase G, insert the tax-revenue function 9.63 into the nominal government budget constraint 9.60 and divide by price P. Finally, use 9.1 and 9.2 to write $I \equiv g_S S$, insert all that into the goods-market equilibrium condition 9.65, factor out $(1 - T)X$, use 9.11 to write PX as Y, and write the rate of growth of physical capital stock

$$g_S \equiv \frac{I}{S} = \frac{X - (C + G)}{S} = \frac{(1 - T)AX}{S} \tag{9.100}$$

where A was defined in 9.96. The key to our analysis of accommodating and nonaccommodating fiscal policies will be the rate of growth of that rate of growth—that is, the rate of acceleration of physical capital stock

$$g_{gS} = g_A + g_X - g_S \tag{9.101}$$

So far, the employment fraction λ is not a function of time: $g_\lambda = 0$. In that case, insert 9.57 into the production function 9.7, differentiate the latter with respect to time, and find

$$g_X = g_a + \alpha g_F + \beta g_S \tag{9.102}$$

Insert 9.102 into 9.101 and find the rate of acceleration of physical capital stock

$$g_{gS} = g_A + \alpha(g_a/\alpha + g_F - g_S) \tag{9.103}$$

2. An Accommodating Fiscal Policy

Consider an economy finding itself in the steady-state equilibrium growth defined by solutions 9.67 through 9.91. Define an accommodating fiscal policy as one upholding solutions 9.76 and 9.80:

$$g_M = g_{Qb} = g_Y \qquad (9.76, 9.80)$$

The expression A as defined in 9.96 contains the ratios M/Y and Q_b/Y and nothing else that is a function of time. Consequently, A will be stationary if and only if M/Y and Q_b/Y will be. By definition 9.76 and 9.80 they will be; consequently A will be stationary:

$$g_A = 0$$

and the Solow (1956) convergence proof will apply. In equation 9.103 there will then be only three possibilities: if $g_S > g_a/\alpha + g_F$ then $g_{gS} < 0$. If

$$g_S = g_a/\alpha + g_F \qquad (9.104)$$

then $g_{gS} = 0$. Finally, if $g_S < g_a/\alpha + g_F$, then $g_{gS} > 0$. Consequently, if greater than equation 9.104, g_S is falling; if equal to 9.104, g_S is stationary; and if less than 9.104, g_S is rising. Furthermore, g_S cannot alternate around 9.104, because differential equations trace continuous time paths, and as soon as a g_S-path touched 9.104 it would have to stay there. Finally, g_S cannot converge to anything else than 9.104; if it did, by letting enough time elapse we could make the left-hand side of 9.103 smaller than any arbitrarily assignable positive constant ε, however small, without the same being possible for the right-hand side. We conclude that g_S must either equal $g_a/\alpha + g_F$ from the outset or, if it does not, converge to that value.

Insert Equation 9.104 into 9.102 and find the rate of growth of physical output

$$g_X = g_S$$

which was indeed our steady-state equilibrium-growth solution 9.85.

As we just saw, under an accommodating fiscal policy, the expression A as defined in 9.96 will remain stationary. As a result, the aftertax real rate of interest 9.96 will also remain stationary, and there will be neither crowding out nor crowding in.

3. Nonaccommodating Fiscal Policies

Our solutions 9.67 through 9.91 defined infinitely many steady-state equilibrium growth tracks, each with its own employment fraction λ and inflationary potential p. Once settled on any of them, the economy will tend to stay on it. As we saw in section 9.VI.2, on such a track, expectations will be self-fulfilling, and self-fulfilling expectations are not abandoned easily.

Could a nonaccommodating fiscal policy switch the economy from one such steady-state equilibrium growth track to another deemed more desirable by the policymaker? In trying to answer that question we can expect no help from our solutions 9.67 through 9.91. They hold for steady-state equilibrium growth tracks but are silent on how to switch from one track to another. We are condemned to the use of intuition.

Once we switch from one track to another, we must allow the employment fraction λ to vary with time. In that case we must insert 9.57 into the production function 9.7, differentiate the latter with respect to time, treat λ as a variable, and find

$$g_X = g_a + \alpha g_\lambda + \alpha g_F + \beta g_s \qquad (9.105)$$

Once we switch from one track to another, we shall take people by surprise. Expectations are no longer self-fulfilling. In that case, the timing of events will be crucial. The immediate effects of a nonaccommodating fiscal policy will set the tone of the switching operation. Let us distinguish between Keynesian and monetarist versions of a nonaccommodating fiscal policy.

4. An Expansionary (Keynesian) Fiscal Policy: Crowding Out

Keynesians will wish to switch the economy from a low-employment track to a high-employment track. They are inclined to use the income mechanism and will do it by raising government purchase and fiscal deficit.

Define a nonaccommodating expansionary fiscal policy as one replacing our solutions 9.76 and 9.80: $g_M = g_{Qb} = g_Y$ by the inequality

$$g_M, g_{Qb} > g_Y \qquad (9.106)$$

The expression A as defined in 9.96 will be changing if and only if M/Y and Q_b/Y are changing. By the definition 9.106 M/Y and Q_b/Y are growing. For as long as they are, A will keep declining:

$$g_A < 0$$

Now according to 9.96 the aftertax real rate of interest ρ, on which investment depends, is in inverse proportion to A. And according to 9.26

and 9.96 the investment fraction I/X in an economy knowing government is in direct proportion to A. No doubt a declining A means crowding out. But first the employment fraction λ, now free to vary, may rise.

5. Crowding Out Delayed

One part of the immediate impact of the nonaccommodating policy occurs in the bond market. Bonds themselves purchase no goods; only money does. Not until sold can a bond issue finance anything. The expansionary policy will allow larger bond issues than an accommodating policy would have done. Disturbing an equilibrium of accommodation, such government invasion of the bond market will generate excess supply.

The other part of the immediate impact occurs in the goods market. The expansionary policy will allow a larger deficit, hence larger physical government purchase G, than an accommodating policy would have done. Disturbing an equilibrium of accommodation, such a larger purchase will generate excess demand in the goods market, temporarily met by inventory depletion. The government disbursement of more money will generate excess supply in the money market. Those unwilling to hold more money at the existing interest rate will buy bonds. Such spillover excess demand for bonds will meet the excess supply generated by the government invasion of the bond market, and any net effect upon the price Π_b of bonds will be small.

As a result, the immediate impact in the money and bond markets may be overshadowed by the impact in the goods market. Here, the unforeseen inventory depletion will be read as a signal to hire labor to restore a normal inventory ratio. The employment fraction λ, now a function of time, is growing. In 9.105 the term αg_λ will be positive and in 9.101 may neutralize the negative g_A. In that case, the larger physical government purchase is not crowding out anything but simply raising the employment fraction λ.

The growing employment fraction is moving the economy up an ever-steeper Phillips hyperbola 9.58. If inflation would accelerate for long enough to raise $g_Y = g_P + g_X$ to equality with the initially raised policy instruments g_M and g_{Qb}, rigidly adhered to, then our solutions 9.76 and 9.80 would have been restored. If they are not, the policymaker himself may of course at any time deliberately restore them by lowering g_M and g_{Qb} to equality with whatever value of g_Y has been reached.

After such a return to an accommodating fiscal policy the economy may, with luck, have been switched to a different steady-state equilibrium growth track satisfying 9.67 through 9.91 and having a higher λ and with it a higher g_P and g_w. If so, a higher employment fraction has been achieved but only accompanied by a higher rate of inflation. The new growth track would have a permanently lowered A and hence a permanently lowered investment fraction of output $(1 - T)A$; a permanently raised after-tax real rate of interest 9.96; a permanently lowered capital coefficient 9.25; and a permanently lowered real wage rate 9.99.

6. Crowding Out Coming Fully into Play

Moving up an ever-steeper Phillips hyperbola 9.58, the policymaker gets less and less of what he wants (abatement of unemployment) and more and more of what he does not want (inflation). If ambitious and impatient, he will refuse to restore accommodation and instead maintain 9.106. As long as he does, M/Y and Q_b/Y will keep growing. As long as they do, A will keep declining, and with it the aftertax real rate of interest 9.96 will keep growing and, according to 9.42, the stock market keep declining. Such ever-growing discouragement of investment will eventually halt and perhaps reverse the growth of the employment fraction λ, and unmodified crowding out will come into play. With a negative g_A no longer neutralized by any positive αg_λ, the rate of acceleration of physical capital stock 9.103 will show that

$$g_{gS} < \alpha(g_a/\alpha + g_F - g_S) \qquad (9.107)$$

Under an accommodating fiscal policy, g_{gS} was equal to $\alpha(g_a/\alpha + g_F - g_S)$ and would become zero when $g_S = g_a/\alpha + g_F$. Now g_{gS} is less than that and will still be negative once $g_S = g_a/\alpha + g_F$ at point A in figure 9–3. But a negative g_{gS} means that g_S is still declining and will keep doing so as it approaches a level, shown as a solid line, below

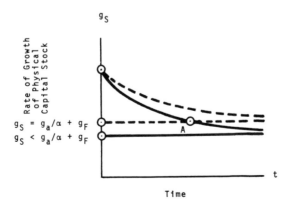

Figure 9–3. An Expansionary Fiscal Policy. Crowding Out

$g_a/\alpha + g_F$. In short: under an expansionary fiscal policy, private physical capital stock will eventually grow less rapidly than at the rate $g_a/\alpha + g_F$, and in this sense there is crowding out. According to 9.99 the growing aftertax real rate of interest will also slow down the growth of the real wage rate and according to 9.8 the growth of labor productivity X/L. We are simulating "the productivity slowdown"!

7. Can A Keynesian Policy Succeed?

The purpose of an expansionary Keynesian fiscal policy was to switch the economy from a low-employment track to a high-employment track. Can it succeed?

   If halted and replaced by an accommodating fiscal policy before crowding out comes fully into play, the Keynesian policy may succeed. Once crowding out comes fully into play the aftertax real rate of interest will keep growing and the stock market keep declining. Such discouragement of investment, we said, might reverse the initial growth of the employment fraction λ, and the Keynesian policy will have failed.

8. A Contractionary (Monetarist) Fiscal Policy:
Crowding In

Monetarists wish to switch the economy from a high-inflation track to a low-inflation track. They are inclined to use the interest mechanism and will do it by reducing government purchase and fiscal deficit, thus making room for private demand.

   Define a nonaccommodating contractionary fiscal policy as one replacing our solutions 9.76 and 9.80: $g_M = g_{Qb} = g_Y$ by the inequality

$$g_M, g_{Qb} < g_Y \qquad\qquad (9.108)$$

   The expression A as defined in 9.96 will be changing if and only if M/Y and Q_b/Y are changing. By the definition 9.108 M/Y and Q_b/Y are declining. For as long as they are, A will keep growing:

$$g_A > 0$$

   Now according to 9.96 the aftertax real rate of interest ρ, on which investment depends, is in inverse proportion to A. And according to 9.26 and 9.96 the investment fraction I/X in an economy knowing government is in direct proportion to A. No doubt a growing A means crowding in. But first the employment fraction λ, now free to vary, may fall.

9. Crowding In Delayed

One part of the immediate impact of the nonaccommodating policy occurs in the bond market. Bonds themselves purchase no goods; only money does. Not until sold can a bond issue finance anything. The contractionary policy will allow smaller bond issues than an accommodating policy would have done. Disturbing an equilibrium of accommodation, such government retreat from the bond market will generate excess demand.

The other part of the immediate impact occurs in the goods market. The contractionary policy will allow a smaller deficit, hence smaller physical government purchase G, than an accommodating policy would have done. Disturbing an equilibrium of accommodation, such a smaller purchase will generate excess supply in the goods market, temporarily met by inventory accumulation. The government disbursement of less money will generate excess demand in the money market. Those unwilling to hold less money at the existing interest rate will sell bonds. Such spillover excess supply of bonds will meet the excess demand generated by the government retreat from the bond market, and any net effect upon the price Π_b of bonds will be small.

As a result, the immediate impact in the money and bond markets may be overshadowed by the impact in the goods market. Here, the unforeseen inventory accumulation will be read as a signal to lay off labor to restore a normal inventory ratio. The employment fraction λ, now a function of time, is declining. In 9.105 the term αg_λ will be negative and in 9.101 may neutralize the positive g_A. In that case, the resources released by the government retreat from the goods market will not generate crowding in but simply go to waste.

The declining employment fraction λ is moving the economy down an ever-flatter Phillips hyperbola 9.58. If inflation would decelerate for long enough to lower $g_Y = g_P + g_X$ to equality with the initially lowered policy instruments g_M and g_{Qb}, rigidly adhered to, then our solutions 9.76 and 9.80 would have been restored. If they are not, the policymaker himself may of course at any time deliberately restore them by raising g_M and g_{Qb} to equality with whatever value of g_Y has been reached.

After such a return to an accommodating fiscal policy, the economy may, with luck, have been switched to a different steady-state equilibrium growth track satisfying 9.67 through 9.91 and having a lower λ and with it a lower g_P and g_w. If so, permanently less inflation has been accomplished. But unless the inflationary potential p has been reduced, less inflation is accompanied by a lower employment fraction λ. The new growth track would have a permanently raised A and hence a permanently raised investment fraction of output $(1 - T)A$; a permanently lowered aftertax real rate of interest 9.96; a permanently raised capital coefficient 9.25; and a permanently raised real wage rate 9.99.

10. Crowding In Coming Fully into Play

Moving down an ever-flatter Phillips hyperbola 9.58, the policymaker gets
less and less of what he wants (abatement of inflation) and more and more of
what he does not want (unemployment). If ambitious and impatient, he will
refuse to restore accommodation and instead maintain 9.108. As long as he
does, M/Y and Q_b/Y will keep declining. As long as they do, A will keep
growing, and with it the aftertax real rate of interest 9.96 will keep declining
and, according to 9.42 the stock market keep rising. Such ever-growing
encouragement of investment will eventually halt and perhaps reverse the
decline of the employment fraction λ, and unmodified crowding in will come
into play. With a positive g_A no longer neutralized by any negative αg_λ, the
rate of acceleration of physical capital stock 9.103 will show that

$$g_{gS} > \alpha(g_a/\alpha + g_F - g_S) \tag{9.109}$$

Under an accommodating fiscal policy, g_{gS} was equal to $\alpha(g_a/\alpha +
g_F - g_S)$ and would become zero when $g_S = g_a/\alpha + g_F$. Now g_{gS} is greater
than that and will still be positive once $g_S = g_a/\alpha + g_F$ at point B in
figure 9–4. But a positive g_{gS} means that g_S is still growing and will keep
doing so as it approaches a level, shown as a solid line, above $g_a/\alpha + g_F$.
In short: under a contractionary fiscal policy, private physical capital stock
will eventually grow more rapidly than at the rate $g_a/\alpha + g_F$, and in this
sense there is crowding in.

11. Can A Monetarist Policy Succeed?

The purpose of a contractionary monetarist fiscal policy was to switch the
economy from a high-inflation track to a low-inflation track. Can it succeed?

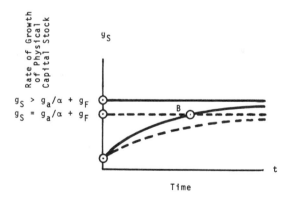

Figure 9–4. A Contractionary Fiscal Policy. Crowding In

The trick, monetarists say, is to break inflationary expectations. Having Eckstein's three inflation components in it, our Phillips function 9.58 will help us finding a precise meaning of the vague term "breaking inflationary expectations." If taken literally the term "breaking inflationary expectations" would merely mean reducing the g_P of the second term of the Phillips function 9.58 and would accomplish nothing of permanence: as long as nothing had changed on the right-hand side of our solution 9.77, expected g_P would simply have been depressed below its equilibrium value 9.77. Expectations would no longer be self-fulfilling, and in the long run, the equilibrium value 9.77 would prevail.

For anything of permanence to be accomplished, the right-hand side of our solution 9.77 must be reduced—by reducing either the employment fraction λ or the inflationary potential p. As for the employment fraction λ, a contractionary monetarist fiscal policy may initially reduce it—as we just saw. But if crowding in did come fully into play, the aftertax real rate of interest would keep declining and the stock market keep rising. Such encouragement of investment, we said, might reverse the initial decline of the employment fraction λ.

The only remaining hope of permanently reducing the right-hand side of our solution 9.77 must lie in a permanent reduction of the inflationary potential p, Eckstein's shock component. The positive oil shock of 1974 and 1979 gave us inflation rates close to ten percent, see figure 2–2. A similar but negative shock, generated this time by a contractionary monetarist fiscal policy, might permanently reduce our equilibrium rate of inflation 9.77, including self-fulfilling expectations.

Such must be the precise meaning of the vague term "breaking inflationary expectations."

12. The Special Case of a Balanced Budget at Zero Inflation

As we saw in section 9.IV.6, zero inflation is at least thinkable. Some of our steady-state equilibrium growth tracks are indeed zero-inflation tracks. Let the economy have been successfully switched to such a track. Policy has successfully overcome all obstacles and suppressed everybody's long-run inflationary expectations. Our solution 9.77 has collapsed to zero and with it our solution 9.89 to

$$g_Y = g_X \qquad\qquad (9.110)$$

Would a balanced budget allow the economy to grow along its zero-inflation track? The answer is no. Our economy is a closed one in which money and bonds can come into existence in no other way than by financing a government budget deficit. Conversely, a government budget deficit can be financed in no other way than by expanding the money and bond supplies. In other words, a balanced budget means frozen money and bond supplies:

$$g_M = g_{Qb} = 0 \qquad (9.111)$$

Assume that, in accordance with our solution 9.88, $g_X > 0$. Then as long as 9.110 and 9.111 are holding, 9.108 will hold. A balanced budget is contractionary and will not allow the economy to stay on its zero-inflation track. This result may surprise those whose reasoning is static.

IX. Conclusions

As we did in chapter 7, we have used a neoclassical growth model to trace the effect of investment on physical capital stock and to relate the flow of physical output to physical capital stock. As we did in chapter 8, we have optimized physical capital stock. Optimization involves discounting future cash flows. The rate to be applied when discounting them is the aftertax nominal rate of interest. We have applied it and derived expressions for desired physical capital stock and investment. Those expressions helped us find the equilibrium level of the aftertax real rate of interest and see its sensitivity to inflation and taxation. Comparing a more and a less inflationary steady-state equilibrium growth track, we found the more inflationary track to have the higher aftertax real rate of interest. Comparing a high-tax and a low-tax steady-state equilibrium growth track, we found the high-tax track to have the higher aftertax real rate of interest. Thus did our model display a Feldstein Effect.

Unlike chapter 8 but following Turnovsky, this chapter has kept records of financial assets and liabilities of firms and households and of the budget constraints under which firms and households operate. Corporate shares and government bonds existed side by side and allowed us to identify winners and losers in the inflation game.

Unlike chapter 8, this chapter introduced a labor market and saw the price-wage spiral as an interaction between a price and a wage equation. In two respects monetarist doctrine found no support in our neoclassical-growth setting. First, the rate of inflation was found to be not normally "accelerationist" but to be unique, stationary, and stable as long as the coefficient ϕ of labor's inflationary expectations in the Phillips function was less than unity. Second, the "natural" rate of unemployment was found not to be unique.

Accommodating fiscal policy was defined as adherence to our steady-state growth solutions and nonaccommodating fiscal policy as deviations from them. The consequences of such deviations for crowding out and crowding in via the aftertax real rate of interest were briefly examined. Even under zero inflation, a balanced budget would be nonaccommodating—that is, contractionary.

Notes

1. This comparison must be modified for countries taxing capital gains. According to *The Economist*, Oct. 4, 1980, long-term capital gains were tax-exempt in Australia, Belgium, Holland, Italy, Japan, and West Germany but were taxed at a maximum rate of 15 percent in France, 22 percent in Canada, 28 percent in the United States, and 30 percent in the United Kingdom.

2. "Money is printed paper; when paper loses its value no genuine values are lost. They merely change hands" (my translation).

3. The numerical values are consistent in the sense that ρ will equal 0.05 whether expressed by 9.21 or 9.96. The values are empirically not implausible. For example, in an economy knowing government and inflation, the investment fraction of output will be $(1 - T)A$ and equal 0.06. In an economy not knowing government and inflation, the overall propensity to save will be the first term of A, $1 - (\alpha c_1 + \beta c_2)$, and equal 0.09. Government and inflation, then, reduce the investment fraction from 0.09 to 0.06! For another example, the work money does is to transact $Y + iQ_b$; hence, the velocity of money is $(Y + iQ_b)/M$. Divide numerator and denominator by Y and see that the velocity of money is nothing but our bond-money ratio $(1 + iQ_b/Y)/(M/Y)$ and will equal 6.023.

References

A. S. Blinder and R. M. Solow, "Analytical Foundations of Fiscal Policy," *The Economics of Public Finance* (Brookings), Washington, D.C., 1974.

O. Eckstein, *Core Inflation*, Englewood Cliffs, N.J., 1981.

M. Feldstein, "Inflation, Income Taxes, and the Rate of Interest: A Theoretical Analysis," *Amer. Econ. Rev.*, Dec. 1976, *66*, 809–820.

I. Fisher, *The Theory of Interest*, New York, 1930.

M. Friedman, "The Role of Monetary Policy," *Amer. Econ. Rev.*, Mar. 1968, *58*, 1–17.

G. Mann, *Deutsche Geschichte 1919–1945*, Frankfurt am Main, 1961.

A. W. Phillips, "The Relation between Unemployment and the Rate of Change of Money Wage Rates in the United Kingdom, 1851–1957," *Economica*, Nov. 1958, *25*, 283–299.

R. M. Solow, "A Contribution to the Theory of Economic Growth," *Quart. J. Econ.*, Feb. 1956, *70*, 65–94.

J. Tobin and W. Buiter, "Long-Run Effects of Fiscal and Monetary Policy on Aggregate Demand," J. L. Stein (ed.), *Monetarism. Studies in Monetary Economics 1*, Amsterdam, 1976.

S. J. Turnovsky, *Macroeconomic Analysis and Stabilization Policy*, Cambridge, 1977.

———, "Macroeconomic Dynamics and Growth in a Monetary Economy," *J. Money, Credit, and Banking*, Feb. 1978, *10*, 1–26.

———, "Monetary and Fiscal Policy in a Long-Run Macroeconomic Model," *Econ. Record*, June 1980, *56*, 158–170.

**Part IV
The End**

10 Conclusions and Reality

Events do not happen in categories—economic, intellectual, military—they happen in sequence. —Barbara Tuchman (1981:70)

Part I. The Setting

Chapter 1. Fiscal History

The three chapters of part I provide a bare minimum of background—historical, statistical, and theoretical. Chapter 1 shows that in the United States the long-term growth of government purchases of goods and services has been roughly steady-state. The two world wars represent the only major deviations from steady-state growth. They also represent major government deficits. Government must finance deficits by issuing money and bonds. The money supply and government debt of the United States and its primary adversary in two world wars were traced back to World War One. New major deficits arose in the late 1970s, absorbing substantial percentages of net private saving.

Chapter 2. Six Macroeconomic Functions

Rather than recording events as they happen in sequence, Chapter 2 tried to see them in categories. For the seventeen turbulent years from 1965 to 1981, unsophisticated scatter diagrams were drawn of six familiar macroeconomic behavior functions, Keynesian and monetarist. Simplified linearized versions of them were used to build the short-run fiscal-policy models of chapters 5 and 6.

Chapter 3. Early Macroeconomic Theory

All theory is simplification, and our crudest simplification is macroeconomic theory. Chapter 3 identified two schools of thought—that is, unemployment theory and inflation theory—that have asserted themselves with varying weights over the past three centuries. The chapter traced Keynesian unemployment theory to Petty, Mun, Yarranton, Steuart, Lauderdale, and Ohlin and monetarist inflation theory to Hume, Turgot, Say, Ricardo, Wicksell, and Fisher.

Part II. The Short Run

Chapter 4. Keynesian Statics

Part II began by simulating Keynesians within the static framework of frozen prices. The first half of chapter 4 specified and solved an algebraic Keynesian model in which the policy instruments were the fiscal deficit and the tax rate and in which physical output was the sole equilibrating variable. Adjustment of saving to autonomous deficit and investment, then, had to be brought about by adjustment of physical output alone, leaving no room for crowding out.

That was an extreme and special case. History's earliest and purest example of it was the quantity expansion brought about in Nazi Germany in the 1933–1936 period by a three-armed fiscal policy. The first arm was a succession of large budget deficits. Figure 1–4 showed the 50 percent increase in German federal debt over the three years. The second arm was tax reduction in the form of, first, tax credit for investment in import-substituting processes; second, up to 40 percent tax credit for indirect taxes paid; third, accelerated depreciation—down to one year—of machines, tools, and utility vehicles; and, fourth, excise-tax exemption for motor vehicles and other items of military interest. The third arm was public works in the form of a system of interstate expressways meeting, almost perfectly, Sir William Petty's prescription from 1662: They were "works of much labor and little art"; they were "without expence of Foreign Commodities"; and they were "High-wayes so broad, firm, and eaven, as whereby the charge and tedium of travelling and Carriages may be greatly lessened"—and mobilization for a two-front war greatly facilitated! After 1935 the emphasis shifted to open rearmament.

The architect of such Keynesian practice without Keynesian theory was Hjalmar Horace Greeley Schacht, president of the central bank but equipped with powers only a dictatorship could bestow. His results were impressive. Figure 7–1 showed Germany's early upturn compared with the United States. Not until 1936, when Keynes' *General Theory* finally arrived, did labor shortage, crowding out, and inflation become noticeable.[1]

Thirty years later, something similar proved equally successful in a democracy. Our accelerated depreciation of 1962, first tried in 1954; our investment tax credit of 1962; and our reductions of corporate and personal income-tax rates of 1964 were leaves borrowed from Schacht's book, although the Council of Economic Advisers may not have known it. One parallel was missing—that is, the large Schachtian deficits. The unusually high and steady growth rate of the period, seen in figure 7–1, generated enough tax revenue to avoid them. Blinder-Solow (1974:24) have observed that at the time, the United States succeeded in ironing out more cyclical fluctuation than any other major industrial country and that nearly two-thirds of the accomplishment was due to the automatic stabilizers. As in the 1930s, inflation seemed far from being a danger. Its demand component was low. Throughout the first half of the 1960s, the unemployment rate was above both the normal for the United States and the normal for other major industrial countries. The shock component was even negative. Energy and food prices were edging lower.

The 1960–1965 period may have been the last time orthodox Keynesianism worked. Even before that, Hicks (1956:150) had warned that

> The world of the thirties, which was Keynesian for one reason—because the working of the price-mechanism was so largely suspended by Depression—was succeeded by the world of the forties which was Keynesian for quite another reason—because the price-mechanism was superseded by controls. In both of these worlds the Keynesian model was at home. But one has a feeling that the world of the fifties is not Keynesian in either of these ways; it may be Keynesian in its policies, but it is not Keynesian in its working.

With physical output as its sole equilibrating variable, the model of the first half of chapter 4 left no room for crowding out. The last half of chapter 4 used the familiar static *IS-LM* framework to introduce an additional equilibrating variable, the rate of interest. Crowding out became possible but prices remained frozen.

Chapter 5. Inflation: A Nonaccommodating Policy

Chapters 5 and 6 gave up the static framework of frozen prices and offered models of two fiscal policies under inflation—a nonaccommodating and an accommodating one, respectively.

Any model including the rate of inflation $g_P \equiv (dP/dt)/P$ among its equilibrating variables will contain the derivative with respect to time dP/dt; hence it will be intrinsically dynamic. But the two models were merely semidynamic. They did not attempt to trace the effect of investment upon physical capital stock, use a production function relating the flow of physical output to physical capital stock, or optimize the latter. Being intrinsically dynamic, if only semidynamic, both models determined the rates of change of their solutions for four equilibrating variables: the nominal rate of interest, physical output, the real rate of interest, and the rate of inflation.

The purpose of chapter 5 was to revisit the balanced budget and see it in an inflationary setting. The nominal rate of interest, physical output, and the rate of inflation were found to be declining but the real rate of interest to be growing. The reason was that the frozen nominal money and bond supplies required by the balanced budget would, under inflation, mean declining real money and bond supplies. But if no equilibrating variable became stationary, fiscal equilibrium should no longer be defined as a situation with a balanced budget. A better definition should be found.

Chapter 6. Inflation: An Accommodating Policy

Chapter 6 used the same variables and equations as chapter 5 but did not require the budget to be balanced. With this restriction lifted, chapter 6 found new solutions and their rates of change. Those rates of change were zero in the special case that the rates of growth of the money and bond supplies were equal and in turn equal to the rate of growth of price. Such a case of fiscal accommodation was an equilibrium in the sense that all motion had come to an end and that all expectations were self-fulfilling. Did such an equilibrium exist? The system was quadratic in the nominal rate of interest; hence it had two roots and two fiscal-accommodation equilibria, one displaying deflation and a fiscal surplus and one displaying inflation and a fiscal deficit. The rates of change of our solutions enabled us to examine the motion around these equilibria and to conclude that they were stable. In all such motion, physical output and the rate of inflation always moved in unison. As a result, anything that reduced the rate of inflation by one percentage point would always increase the rate of excess capacity by roughly four percentage points.

Part III. The Long Run

Chapter 7. Neoclassical Growth

Ultimately, the book wants to see fiscal policy in its natural habitat—that of a growing economy. Only full long-run dynamics can do that. To provide a suitable framework, chapter 7 restated and solved a neoclassical growth model—so far without government in it. The solutions possessed five important properties, all confronted with historical reality: (1) convergence to steady-state growth of output; (2) identical steady-state growth rates of output and capital stock but not of labor and capital stock; (3) stationary rate of return to capital; (4) identical steady-state growth rates of the real wage rate and labor productivity; and (5) stationary distributive shares. None of the five properties was found to be seriously at odds with historical reality.

Chapter 8. Monetarist Long-Run Dynamics

Monetarists wish to include the rate of inflation among their equilibrating variables. Any model admitting inflation as an equilibrating variable will contain a derivative with respect to time, hence will be dynamic, and will contain two additional equilibrating variables—the nominal and the real rate of interest. Consequently, a monetarist model must be a dynamic two-interest-rates model. According to Friedman, monetary policy cannot peg the rate of unemployment for more than very limited periods. Consequently, a monetarist model must dismiss and go beyond such limited periods and become a long-run model.

A long-run, dynamic, two-interest-rates model is obviously incompatible with the short-run, static, one-interest-rate *IS-LM* framework offered by Friedman (1970) himself as his "theoretical framework." As Thygesen (1977) observed in his Nobel article, Friedman "is clearly uncomfortable with it." He should be!

More successfully, chapter 8 offered a neoclassical steady-state growth model capable of delivering most of Friedman's conclusions. His growth-*rate* conclusions were delivered impeccably. No growth-rate solution for a real variable included the rate of growth of the money supply. All growth-rate solutions for nominal variables included the rate of growth of the money supply. His growth-*level* conclusions—that money shouldn't matter for the level of real variables—were not delivered. Comparing a more and a less inflationary steady-state equilibrium growth track, we did find the more inflationary track to have the higher level of the aftertax real rate of interest. But monetarists cannot have it both ways. They gave us the crowding-out concept. In our model, money could not come into existence in any other way than by financing a government budget deficit. In the monetarist view, such deficits produce crowding out, and how could they, except via a higher aftertax real rate of interest?

Chapter 9. Full Long-Run Dynamics

The purpose of chapter 9 was to explore a full steady-state growth fiscal equilibrium within the framework of an extended neoclassical growth model. The model made room for the assets, liabilities, and budget constraints of firms, households, and government. Deficits must be financed. Firms financed theirs by supplying claims on themselves in the form of dividend-bearing shares. Households saved; hence, they supplied no claims on themselves but demanded claims on firms and government. As in our previous chapters, government financed its deficit by supplying claims on itself in the form of noninterest-bearing money and interest-bearing bonds.

The original neoclassical growth model traced the effect of investment on physical capital stock and used a production function relating the flow of physical output to physical capital stock but made no attempt to optimize the latter. Such an attempt was made in chapters 8 and 9. Optimization of physical capital stock involved maximization of present net worth. Present net worth of an asset was defined as its present gross worth minus its price of acquisition. Present gross worth was found by discounting the future cash flows generated by the asset. The discount rate used was crucial. The discount rate used must reflect the cost of capital faced by the firm, and that cost is affected by taxation.

We had to include taxation, then, but tried to keep it as simple as possible. Money national income was taxed once and at a uniform rate. Capital gains were tax-exempt. Interest expense was tax-deductible. Four practically important features of the U. S. tax structure escaped our model. First, the assumption of immortal capital stock removed depreciation from the model and with it the heavier tax burden under inflation and historical-cost depreciation. Second, the double taxation of corporate profits escaped us. So did, third, the taxation of nominal and realized capital gains, and, fourth, differential personal-income tax rates. Even so, the effect of taxation on optimization came through. We found desired physical capital stock and investment to be in inverse proportion to the aftertax real rate of interest ρ.

But ρ was not merely the aftertax real rate of interest. To see what else it was, we determined the prices of bonds and shares. The price of a bond was found to be a capitalization of its current before-tax interest payment, and the capitalization factor was $1/r$ or the reciprocal of the before-tax nominal rate of interest. The price of a share was found to be a capitalization of its current dividend payment, and the capitalization factor was $1/\rho$ or the reciprocal of the aftertax real rate of interest. It followed that ρ was also the dividend yield—the cost of equity capital faced by the firm. When priced at such prices, bonds and shares were found to yield the same rate of aftertax real return. That rate was ρ.

Chapter 9. Steady-State Equilibrium Growth Solutions

Our system implied self-fulfilling expectations; we used the same symbol for the expected and realized values of any variable, implying equality between the two. Was such equality always possible? It was if the system had a set of solutions. A set of explicit steady-state growth-rate solutions 9.67 through 9.91 was found for the twenty-five variables of the system—that is, the money wage rate; the price of goods; the nominal rate of interest; the after-tax real rate of interest; physical consumption, investment, government purchase, and output; labor employed; physical capital stock and marginal productivity of capital stock; the demand for and supply of money, bonds, and shares; the dividend payment per share; the price of bonds and shares; money national income; tax revenue; money disposable income; and the wage and profits bills.

The set of solutions 9.67 through 9.91 defined infinitely many steady-state equilibrium growth tracks. Each track had its own employment fraction λ, which was Eckstein's state of demand (1981). Each track had its own inflationary potential p, which was Eckstein's shock. All tracks had a common core defined by Eckstein (1981:8) as "the rate that would occur on the economy's long-term growth path, provided the path were free of shocks, and the state of demand were neutral in the sense that markets were in long-run equilibrium."

Of solutions in which the employment fraction λ and the inflationary potential p were present, there were infinitely many. We found λ and p present in the growth-rate solutions for the thirteen nominal variables of the system. But some growth-rate solutions *were* unique. We found λ and p absent from the growth-rate solutions for the twelve real variables of the system. The λ and p were also absent from the growth-rate solution for the real wage rate. For any value of the employment fraction λ, the real wage rate was growing at the same rate. Any value, in other words, of the unemployment fraction $1 - \lambda$ was a Friedmanian natural rate! Friedman's natural rate was not unique. Its lack of uniqueness helped us modify simple monetarist notions about crowding out and crowding in.

Chapter 9. The Price-Wage Spiral

Chapter 9 saw the price-wage spiral as an interaction between a price and a wage equation. The price equation was a derivation of the mark-up pricing often overlooked but inherent in a neoclassical model: price equals per-unit labor cost marked up in the proportion $1/\alpha$ where α is labor's exponent in a Cobb-Douglas production function.

The wage equation was an expectations-augmented Phillips function. The size of the coefficient ϕ of labor's inflationary expectations turned out to be crucial. The rate of inflation was found to be unique, stationary, and stable only as long as the coefficient ϕ was less than unity. For ϕ approaching unity, we found, unlike Turnovsky (1977:177), an indeterminate rate of inflation—possibly hyperinflation or hyperdeflation. For ϕ greater than unity, we found the rate of inflation to be unique, stationary but unstable.

In the real world, then, how large is ϕ? Surveying 1963–1975 inflation theory, Frisch (1977) reported that most empirical work has found $\phi < 1$, that Gordon (1976) was unable to reject the hypothesis that $\phi = 1$ after 1971, and that ϕ may vary procyclically. Maybe there is a structural rather than a cyclical change in ϕ. Using a dummy to allow a regression coefficient to change, Eckstein (1981:77–79) found a statistically significant break occurring in 1974. For the 1956–1973 interval his coefficients of short-term and long-term price expectations had a sum not significantly different from unity. For the 1974–1980 interval, they summed to 0.63, significantly different from unity. A possible explanation is the growth of the nonunionized segment of the labor market (sunbelt, nonwhites, and women) at the expense of the unionized segment.

Monetarists imagine a vertical long-run Phillips function. Ours looked like a rectangular hyperbola (and was one if its $\pi = -1$). It also looked like Eckstein's empirical Phillips curve (1981:47–48) whose upper branch is so steep that at unemployment rates below 6 percent there "is virtually no trade-off," and whose lower branch is so flat that the achievement of a 6 percent inflation rate "requires the maintenance of near depression conditions."

Chapter 9. Winners and Losers in the Inflation Game

The financial stock-flow bookkeeping applied in chapter 9 was used to identify winners and losers in the inflation game. In steady-state equilibrium growth, firms were neither winners nor losers. Their investment was matched by new equity of the same value, and the appreciation of existing equity was matched by inflation. According to our solution 9.79 the rates of growth of share and goods prices would be the same. Figure 9–2 showed an extreme case. In the German hyperinflation, share prices followed goods prices quite accurately.

Households were losers in the sense that on capital account they suffered real capital losses on their money and bond holdings and made neither real capital gains nor losses on their share holdings. All expectations being self-fulfilling, however, all real capital gains and losses were fully anticipated and portfolios adjusted accordingly.

Government was a winner in the sense that on capital account it made real capital gains on its money and bond liabilities—matching the real capital losses of households. Figure 1–4 showed an extreme case: The German hyperinflation wiped out the entire war debt.[2]

Chapter 9. Steady-State Equilibrium Level Solutions

In steady-state growth theory, it is usually easier to find solutions for growth rates than for levels. But our expressions for desired physical capital stock and investment helped us solve for the equilibrium level of the aftertax real rate of interest ρ or, which was the same thing, the dividend yield and see its sensitivity to inflation and taxation. Comparing a more and a less inflationary steady-state equilibrium growth track, we found the more inflationary track to have the higher aftertax real rate of interest. Comparing a high-tax and a low-tax steady-state equilibrium growth track, we found the high-tax track to have the higher aftertax real rate of interest.

The sensitivity of the aftertax real rate of interest was small but magnified itself into the sensitivity of both a nominal and a real variable. The nominal one was the before-tax nominal rate of interest r. The real one was the required physical marginal productivity κ of capital stock. If κ had to be higher, desired capital stock and investment would have to be smaller. Thus did our model display a Feldstein Effect (1976).

Having examined the level of the aftertax real rate of interest, we examined two important ratios depending on it: the capital coefficient and the real wage rate.

Chapter 9. Nonsteady-State Growth: Crowding Out and Crowding In

An accommodating fiscal policy was defined as adherence to our steady-state growth solutions 9.67 through 9.91 and a nonaccommodating policy as deviations from them. Our solutions 9.67 through 9.91 defined infinitely many steady-state equilibrium growth tracks, each with its own employment fraction λ and inflationary potential p. Could a nonaccommodating fiscal policy switch the economy from one such steady-state equilibrium growth track to another deemed more desirable by the policymaker? Two nonaccommodating policies were examined.

A Keynesian policymaker might wish to switch the economy from a low-employment track to a high-employment track. He would be inclined to use the income mechanism and would do it by a nonaccommodating fiscal policy stimulating government demand. Moving up an ever-steeper Phillips hyperbola, the policymaker would find himself getting less and less of what he wanted (abatement of unemployment) and more and more of what he did not want (inflation). He might or might not reconcile himself to a return to an accommodating policy. If not, full crowding out would come into play, and the Keynesian policy would have failed.

A monetarist policymaker, on the other hand, might wish to switch the economy from a high-inflation track to a low-inflation track. He would be inclined to use the interest mechanism and would do it by a nonaccommodating fiscal policy discouraging government demand, thus making room for private demand. Moving down an ever-flatter Phillips hyperbola, the policymaker would find himself getting less and less of what he wanted (abatement of inflation) and more and more of what he did not want (unemployment).

He might or might not reconcile himself to a return to an accommodating policy. If not, full crowding in would come into play.

Could such monetarist anti-inflation policy succeed? Our Phillips function 9.58 had in it Eckstein's distinction between demand, shock, and core inflation and helped us see precisely what must be meant by the vague expression "breaking inflationary expectations." Only a permanent reduction of our inflationary potential p, Eckstein's shock component, could permanently reduce the equilibrum rate of inflation 9.77, including self-fulfilling inflationary expectations.

A special case of a nonaccommodating fiscal policy was a balanced budget at zero inflation. A balanced budget turned out to be contractionary and would not allow the economy to stay on its zero-inflation track—a result that might surprise those whose reasoning is static.

Notes

1. As soon as they did, Schacht (1956) refused to go along with further deficits and was removed from office. In 1945, he was liberated from a concentration camp by U.S. forces. In 1946, he was acquitted at the Nuremberg trials.

2. On fiscal aspects of the German hyperinflation and stabilization, see Haller (1976) and Pfleiderer (1976).

References

A. S. Blinder and R. M. Solow, "Analytical Foundations of Fiscal Policy," *The Economics of Public Finance* (Brookings), Washington, D.C., 1974.

O. Eckstein, *Core Inflation*, Englewood Cliffs, N.J., 1981.

M. Feldstein, "Inflation, Income Taxes, and the Rate of Interest: A Theoretical Analysis," *Amer. Econ. Rev.*, Dec. 1976, 66, 809–820.

M. Friedman, "A Theoretical Framework for Monetary Analysis," *J. Polit. Econ.*, March/April 1970, 78, 193–238.

H. Frisch, "Inflation Theory 1963–1975; A 'Second Generation' Survey," *J. Econ. Lit.*, Dec. 1977, 15, 1289–1317.

R. J. Gordon, "Recent Developments in the Theory of Inflation and Unemployment," *J. Monetary Econ.*, Apr. 1976, 2, 185–219.

H. Haller, "Die Rolle der Staatsfinanzen für den Inflationsprozess," Deutsche Bundesbank (ed.), *Währung und Wirtschaft in Deutschland 1876–1975*, Frankfurt, 1976.

J. R. Hicks, "Methods of Dynamic Analysis," *25 Economic Essays in Honour of Erik Lindahl, 21 November 1956*, Stockholm, 1956, 139–151.

W. Petty, *A Treatise of Taxes and Contributions*, London, 1662.

O. Pfleiderer, "Die Reichsbank in der Zeit der grossen Inflation, die Stabilisierung der Mark und die Aufwertung von Kapitalforderungen," Deutsche Bundesbank (ed.), *Währung und Wirtschaft in Deutschland 1876–1975*, Frankfurt, 1976.

H. H. G. Schacht, *Confessions of "The Old Wizard,"* Boston, 1956.

N. Thygesen, "The Scientific Contributions of Milton Friedman," *Scan. J. Econ., 79,* 1, 1977, 56–98.

B.W. Tuchman, *Practicing History*, New York, 1981.

S. J. Turnovsky, *Macroeconomic Analysis and Stabilization Policy*, Cambridge, 1977.

Index

Unit:
  monetary unit changing, 3
  physical, of shares, 118, 124
United Kingdom, 81–84, 88–90, 101,
  157
United States:
  automatic stabilizers, 163
  capital gains taxed, 157
  consumption function, 15, 17
  government debt, 5
  government purchases of goods and
    services, 3–4
  government surplus or deficit, 3–4,
    8
  growth of gross national product,
    79–80
  growth rate of total factor pro-
    ductivity, 84
  growth rates of labor, capital, and
    output, 81–84
  growth rates of real wage rate and
    labor productivity, 86
  inflation, 12–13, 14
  investment and real rate of interest,
    14–16
  labor's share, 86–90
  money growth and inflation, 101
  money supply, 5
  own rate of return on capital, 84–87
  tax-revenue function, 15–18
  velocity of money and nominal rate of
    interest, 19, 20
Unstable price-wage equilibrium, 135
U. S. Department of Commerce, 4, 5,
  79–81, 91

Validity of economic model, xxi

Variables:
  nominal, 100, 133
  real, 100, 133
Velocity of money, 32, 157; and nominal
  rate of interest, 19, 20
Vertical:
  LM curve, xx
  Phillips curve, xx, 32

Wage:
  bill, 77, 117
  equation, 113, 133
  rate, real, growth parable, 79;
    monetarist long run, 95, 98; full
    long run, 117, 151, 153; sensitive
    to inflation and taxation, 146–147
Walrasian equilibrium, 21, 98
Walras's law, 130
Wealth:
  economy-wide, 137–139
  firms, 116, 136
  government, 128–129, 137
  households, 121–122, 136–137
  in consumption function, 47, 98, 127
West Germany. *See* Germany
Wicksell, K., 21, 30, 31, 35
Winners and losers in inflation game:
  firms, 136
  government, 137
  households, 136–137
Women, 168

Yarranton, A., 24, 35

Zero inflation, 135–136
Zero-sum game, inflation as a, 139

About the Author

Hans Brems has taught at the University of Copenhagen, the University of California at Berkeley, and, as a visiting professor, at the universities of Göttingen, Hamburg, and Kiel in West Germany and the universities of Göteborg, Lund, and Uppsala in Sweden. *Fiscal Theory* grew out of a series of lectures at the Industrial Institute for Economic and Social Research in Stockholm, the universities of Aarhus and Copenhagen in Denmark, and the University of Basel, Switzerland. Brems has testified before the Joint Economic Committee of the U. S. Congress and is a foreign member of the Royal Danish Academy of Sciences and Letters. He has published several articles in each of the following professional journals: *American Economic Review, Econometrica, Economic Journal, History of Political Economy, Quarterly Journal of Economics,* and *Review of Economics and Statistics.* He wrote the article "Economics" in the *Encyclopedia Americana.*

His books include *Product Equilibrium under Monopolistic Competition* (1951), *Output, Employment, Capital, and Growth* (1959, 1973), *Quantitative Economic Theory* (1968), *Labor, Capital, and Growth* (Lexington Books, 1973), *Inflation, Interest, and Growth* (Lexington Books, 1980), and its simultaneous German edition *Dynamische Makrotheorie—Inflation, Zins und Wachstum* (1980).